FIRED?
FIGHT
BACK!

FIRED?
FIGHT
BACK!

The No-Nonsense Guide for the
Newly Fired, Downsized,
Outplaced, Laid Off, and Those
Who Are Worried About It

160101

Insider Secrets From Mr. X

American Management Association

New York • Atlanta • Boston • Chicago • Kansas City • San Francisco • Washington, D.C.
Brussels • Mexico City • Tokyo • Toronto

Library of Congress Cataloging-in-Publication Data

Mr. X.
    Fired? Fight back ! : the no-nonsense guide for the newly fired, downsized, outplaced, laid off, and those who are worried about it : insider secrets from Mr. X.
        p.   cm.
    Includes bibliographical references and index.
    ISBN 0-8144-7875-1
    1. Unemployment—Psychological aspects.   2. Job hunting.
3. Career development.   I. Title.
HD5708.M72   1995
650.14—dc20   94-41126
                                                        CIP

Printing number

10   9   8   7   6   5   4   3   2   1

Contents

Foreword

I have maintained an employment law practice for the past twenty years. Many of my clients are firmly on the management side of the employment ledger until the surprising day when they learn, to their chagrin, that they, too, are employees. That is the day upon which they lose their management fervor and become advocates of just cause.

They become advocates on the day they are fired because it is on that day that they rediscover the principles of fairness and justice in the workplace. The values of fairness and justice, combined with a sense of the worth of the individual, are some of the core, basic values of Americans, and these values ought to be the *guiding* values of our businesses.

However, in many if not most of our American workplaces, employers are granted the judicial presumption to be arbitrary, whimsical, and unfair. The presumption has long outlived its time. The "employment-at-will" presumption is rooted in the laissez-faire, trickle-down economics of the late nineteenth century. There is plenty of academic dispute over whether the employment-at-will presumption correctly reflected America's judicial thought at the time it was proposed, but the theory was eagerly accepted by employers, since it exalted their "property rights" over the rights of their individual employees. In real terms, employment-at-will takes away all of the rights of individual employees, preserving only the "right" to quit employment at any time for any reason, without restriction. But since our Constitution prohibits involuntary servitude anyway, preservation of an employee's "right to quit" is hardly *quid pro quo* for giving an employer an unfettered right to terminate employment with no notice and without any cause or reason whatsoever.

It is quite clearly time for a change.

The alternative to the employment-at-will system is to provide the unorganized work force with the same rights to dismissal only for just cause that the unionized work force now has. An employee could be fired only if just cause existed for doing so.

In fact, were such a systemic change proposed by national legislation, it would be interesting to see which company would be first to line up and proclaim that it needed to retain its right to fire its employees in an arbitrary, whimsical, and capricious manner. Which would be first to tell our Congress that it had to be able to act unfairly in order to preserve its competitive edge in the marketplace?

The National Employment Lawyers Association (advocates for employee rights) is one organization that stands for the just-cause principle. Its members are lawyers who predominantly represent employees, and who believe that just cause must exist before a job termination can be legitimate. Presently, dismissal only for just cause is not the law generally. Often, depending on the particular state, even the best lawyer may be forced to tell an employee that he or she has no legal protection. There is no substitute, however, for knowing whether you have rights, and if so, what they are, in this increasingly complicated area of law.

The above makes it clear, I hope, why I am pleased to write this "Foreword" to *Fired? Fight Back!* First, it is unusual to find such sophisticated advice given to employees rather than to management. Second, because the author of the book believes that the system of employment-at-will is inherently unfair and transfers far too much power to employers, his advice seeks, in a practical manner, to transfer some of that power back to employees. Third, anyone reading his book will be as well prepared as possible for the traumatic event of being fired. Fourth, even employees who will never in their lives be fired would still benefit substantially from the advice given here. Thorough preparation for an anticipated bad event often makes it more probable that the bad event will, in fact, never occur.

People who are terminated from employment often suffer acute feelings of humiliation, embarrassment, and many times, most of all, isolation. These insider secrets from Mr. X will show you that you are not alone. The book will give a sense of power where you would otherwise feel powerless. It will give you the knowledge that you need to deal on an equal footing in one of the most difficult situations you would otherwise face: being fired. And it will give access, if you need it, to those who will take your side and fight for your rights.

I highly recommend this book to any employee.

> Joseph D. Garrison
> Garrison & Arterton
> President, National Employment Lawyers Association

Introduction

These are tough times we live in.

Companies from the size of IBM down to the local machine shop are laying off employees, often for reasons that have nothing to do with performance. International competition gets tougher every year. Whole layers of management get eliminated, and whole factories are closed.

Harper's Index estimates that 11,800 Americans are fired every working day. These events have become so commonplace that new words are forcing their way into our vocabulary. People don't get laid off, they get "riffed," derived from the initials of *reduction in force*. Companies don't cut back, they "downsize" or, even more innocuously, they "resize." But no matter what the euphemism, people are losing their jobs.*

And that isn't all. Companies are being gobbled up by larger domestic and international competitors at an ever increasing rate. Acquisitions and mergers mean that all of a sudden a lot of activities are being duplicated, especially corporate staff roles in finance and human resources. The good news is that acquisitions and mergers can create economies of scale that are good for profits, but this is of little consolation to those who find themselves unemployed in the process. And we have added yet another word to our vocabulary, borrowed from our British cousins: People who lose their jobs in a merger are said to have become "redundant." Pretty ugly stuff.

The reality is that a lot of people get fired. That's a harsh word, but there is no point in sugarcoating the truth. Studies conducted over the years suggest that about 25 percent of American workers will

*From *What Counts: The Complete Harper's Index,* edited by Claris Conn, Ilena Silverman, and the staff of *Harper's Magazine.* Copyright © 1992 by *Harper's Magazine.* Reprinted by permission of Henry Holt and Company, Inc.

be fired at least once in their careers, and recent events suggest that the odds of never getting fired are getting worse rather than better. Just as each of us should constantly be learning and retraining ourselves to keep up with changes in technology and business practices, it seems obvious that we must also prepare ourselves for that moment when we lose our jobs.

Interestingly enough, a large body of evidence suggests that being fired for poor job performance is one of the least likely reasons for losing a job. In their excellent book, *Parting Company*, William Morin and James Cabrera (leaders of the world's largest outplacement firm) say that 60 percent of the people they see have lost their jobs because of cutbacks, mergers, and reorganizations. Various "chemistry"-related reasons are also important; these refer to personality conflicts and differences in style. *Only 6 percent of their outplacement referrals lost their jobs owing to poor performance!* This may understate the rate of performance-related firings a bit in that outplacement firms are most likely to be brought in when larger layoffs take place, but other studies support the notion that the vast majority of people who lose their jobs do so for reasons other than poor performance.

What does this mean for you? It means that you may be doing your job well, working hard, getting good performance evaluations and still be as vulnerable to losing your job as a poorer performer in the next office or at the next computer or at the next stop on the line. It means that you have to open your mind to new ideas and be ready. It means that you need to spend some time *now* thinking about how to act if and when the moment arrives.

Getting fired for whatever reason, fair or unfair, is a process like any other. It involves some legal rules and some practices that seem to have been handed down over the ages, but is subject to the same forces of fashion and whim that affect the rest of our lives. If you don't know the ground rules, you are going to be victimized. And in this day and age, there is no excuse for being a victim. That is the reason for this book.

The idea for writing a book on such a serious subject had been building up for some time, and was triggered by the firing of a close relative who had been performing in an exemplary fashion. He was a senior executive running a business that had been foundering when he arrived and that was prospering under his leadership. His boss, who had failed in his own efforts to run the business, became increasingly jealous over the success of this new leader and finally could not stand the comparison. The boss acted in the only way he felt would ease his embarrassment: He fired his successor.

Idiotic, you say? Absolutely. Fair, you ask? Absolutely not. And did the stupidity of this action or its lack of fairness make the slightest difference in the decision process? It did not. The reality is that people get fired every day. That it happened to a good friend and relative is what spurred this book into print, but it was not a singular event nor even an unusual one. It simply was real life.

The foundations of what you will read in the pages ahead are built on the following underlying assumptions:

1. *Anyone* can get fired. It is the utmost naïveté to assume that you are exempt from this danger.
2. There are signals you can learn to read with considerable accuracy that will enable you to predict if your job is in imminent danger.
3. There are specific steps you can take to prepare yourself for being fired and to protect yourself if it happens.
4. If that terrible day arrives, you need to learn specific behaviors that will minimize the personal damage and maximize the financial outcome.
5. There are relatively well-entrenched practices with regard to severance treatment of fired employees, some grounded in the law but most derived from past practices and your skill at negotiating. You need to know how to handle these very delicate negotiations.
6. In many regards, *you* are the one with the advantage when you are being fired. This is startling to many people, but absolutely true. You need to know how to recognize this and turn it into action and money.
7. There are laws that protect you in many circumstances, and you may have legal redress available. These laws can vary considerably from state to state, and you need to know which of them applies to you.
8. Finally, there are things you should do after you have been fired to make certain that you get what you have been promised and to ensure that your efforts to find a new job are not hindered.

With this book, you can turn a situation fraught with peril into one in which you get what you need and deserve, and certainly a lot more than you would have expected. Read on!

Part One
The Axe

Chapter 1

Danger on the Horizon

Did you ever know anyone who *wasn't* surprised at being fired? I haven't. This is a situation where we tend to get taken by surprise.

I once had an office next to a mid-level executive who constantly missed schedules, was late to meetings, and got performance reviews that stressed the need for improvement in many areas. Michael's productivity was low, and for the previous five years his salary increases had been nominal at best. He had been transferred around several departments with no noticeable change either in his own behavior or in the opinions his bosses had of him. He had been passed over for multiple promotions.

One day, with times in the company a bit tough, and to the surprise of absolutely no one, Michael was fired along with several other underachievers. He was absolutely thunderstruck. Yes, of course he knew that his performance evaluations had been less than stellar. Yes, he knew that others had gotten the promotions. Indeed, on careful examination, it was obvious that he had observed all the gathering storm warnings. But they didn't register, and he completely missed the picture! He saw the warnings as interesting information, not as portents of things to come. He figured that his positive attributes, such as the fact that everyone liked him on a personal level, would outweigh the many criticisms and job failures.

Those of us who knew and liked him were only surprised that it had taken Michael so long to lose his job. In fact, some of the more daring of us had tried to give him some guidance before it happened. Yet he laughed it all off. "Don't take work so seriously. Only real turkeys ever get fired around here. Sam"—his boss of the moment—"would never do that to me." And so on.

It Can't Happen to Me

Here is the simple truth: No one's job is totally safe. The top job in any company, that of the chief executive officer, is well known to be the most precarious. *If the CEO can get fired, what makes you think you can't be?*

You say that you're doing a good job? Perhaps. That you've been working for the company a long time? No doubt. That the company won't fire someone who tries hard and is loyal? Maybe.

But you might as well buy yourself an ostrich costume for Halloween. You absolutely, positively, unequivocally cannot control the fact of your continued employment unless you were smart enough and had enough negotiating leeway to get an employment contract when you started work. In any event, a contract won't guarantee you a job, though it will set out the terms of your departure in a way that protects you. There are forces at work over which you have no influence whatsoever: the economy, your industry, troubles in other parts of your company, capricious bosses, changes in philosophy, acquisitions. There are reasons for getting fired that have never occurred to you—and never will until they land on you like a ton of bricks.

So what are your choices? One is to play the aforementioned ostrich. You can say to yourself that your job is safe under any circumstances, ludicrous as that assumption may be. Or you can say that the forces at work are beyond your control and thus not worth worrying about. Beyond your control they may be, in some cases, but worry about them you must. More intelligently, you can say that you will be able to see the handwriting on the wall and thus prepare yourself. This last point is the critical one.

▼

"From the moment you take the job you're vulnerable. If you don't win, you're going to be fired. If you do win, you've only put off the day you're going to be fired."

—*Leo Durocher, in* Nice Guys Finish Last, *1975. Copyright © 1975 by Leo Durocher. Reprinted by permission of Simon & Schuster, Inc.*

▲

Paying Attention to the Storm Clouds

People who get fired virtually always have advance warning. Sometimes the warnings are subtle and sometimes they are as obvious as the sun coming up in the morning. But almost always they are there. Let's discuss some of the more obvious ones.

Mediocre Performance Reviews

Performance reviews provide the least subtle warnings of all: Your boss is sending you a clear signal that all is not well. This may be as severe as a warning that you will be fired unless certain things either improve or change, or it may be couched in flowery language, but it is in some way a formal message that change must be forthcoming.

Performance appraisals, whether written or oral, are an art form buffeted by many countervailing forces. On the one hand, most bosses do not want to land on you too hard; after all, they want to be nice people, and if your work is terrible that must say something less than positive about their management and training skills too. On the other hand, there is increasing pressure to document the deficiencies of employees so that there will be a "paper trail" of evidence to support a termination, which in turn provides some protection for the company against potential litigation. What you must do, therefore, is:

1. *Read your performance evaluations with extra care.* Ask questions about anything that is not absolutely clear, and presume that unless your boss is sadistic or getting ready to fire you the next day, the wording used in both written and oral performance evaluations is at least 25 percent more positive than the feelings of the person delivering the message.

2. *Look for hidden meanings.* If your boss says that you are "making progress" in an area of deficiency, there still is the question of whether you are making progress as rapidly as your boss would like. If you have been rated "good" on a scale where the measures are "poor, fair, good, excellent, and superior," this is a considerable condemnation in most companies, and you should find out specifically what changes are needed to move you up in the rankings. (This is the equivalent of the old Gentleman's C in the Ivy League universities, where the grades theoretically ranged from A to F but where in fact no one ever got the lower two grades, so that a C was bad news indeed even though it wouldn't flunk you out.)

3. *Ask how the system works.* For example, if you are in a department with thirty other people who do work similar to yours, you should ask how you rank when compared with others. The fact that

all your evaluations say that your work is "good" to "excellent" is dangerous territory indeed if the standard is that all work must be in the "excellent" to "superior" range. You must not let yourself be seduced by the language of the evaluation. Keep in mind that companies work very hard not to insult their employees, so the words used in evaluations inevitably have a positive tone to them. Dig beneath the surface.

4. *Keep in mind that performance reviews are not bulletproof vests.* The world is full of people who got fired within months of a positive performance review and a nice raise. Even the most positive reviews delivered in complete honesty can be obliterated by events.

Company Troubles

Most people lose their jobs because of troubles in the company, not because of inadequate performance. Trouble signs are easy enough to spot. If your company is publicly owned, and thus its financial statements are available for you to see, find out whether it has been losing money in recent quarters. Have these losses been accelerating? Is there a history of rosy financial projections that failed to be met? If so, you must assume that everyone's job is at risk.

How is your company or division doing against the competition? Do you have a new product that isn't doing so well? Are you losing market share? Are all the articles in your industry publications about competitors rather than about your company? What do your salespeople say about what is happening in the competitive environment? If all these questions have the wrong answers, it does not mean that you are about to be fired. But it does mean that the odds in favor of being fired are a lot higher than they would be if your company were growing and prospering.

Here are some other signs that may be early warning indicators, especially in privately owned companies, which do not release their financial figures publicly:

- Suppliers start refusing to ship you product unless they are paid in advance.
- One of your major customers (if you sell your products or services to other organizations) is itself in financial difficulties.
- The public accountants who do your company's books are fired (or even worse, they resign).
- Payroll is late.

- Employees are asked to take unpaid "vacations."
- Employee benefits or perquisites are reduced or eliminated.
- Everyone is asked to submit ideas for reducing expenditures.

Industry Troubles

New technology constantly replaces old technology. Even the very best of the buggy whip companies is long gone, while today the main-frame business that dominated the computer industry for many years is gasping for breath, surviving more from inertia than from any com-pelling economic logic. High-calorie, high-fat-content foods are find-ing it increasingly difficult to compete in a health-conscious world. Aerosol sprays are environmentally destructive and will need to be replaced. Hand-delivery services and the U.S. Postal Service are threatened by the encroachment of inexpensive electronic communi-cations like the facsimile machine and electronic mail.

You need to do a dispassionate analysis of your business. Is the overall consumption of your products decreasing? Does your em-ployer provide a service that the world requires in decreasing amounts? Is your marketplace beginning to be described as "ma-ture"? In this kind of environment, with growth slowing or declining and profit margins being squeezed, pressures build up on manage-ment to increase efficiency and productivity, code words for getting more work out of fewer people, who individually and collectively are paid less money.

No industry is free from these economic forces. The reality of a capitalist economy is that individual industries start out with one company, which inevitably spawns dozens or even hundreds of oth-ers. There were times when there were over fifty automobile compa-nies in the United States, and almost every electronics product cate-gory has had at least thirty or forty start-ups in the early stages of its existence. There used to be thousands of individually owned book-stores and drugstores.

All this changes dramatically over time. Economics of scale come into play not only in manufacturing, but also in advertising expendi-tures and the ability to negotiate for lower-cost raw materials and sup-plies. Virtually all products and services become commoditized; that is, they become relatively undifferentiated and the prices are very close to the cost of manufacturing (or, in the case of services, to the cost of labor). Eventually a few companies emerge as the winners, although a few smaller "boutique" players may survive because of unusually high quality (and typically expensive) products or because of a very focused niche marketing strategy. And what we are left with is three American automobile companies, very few steel companies, a handful of disk-drive companies, and a bookstore industry dominated by a few big chains.

The implications of this for you are obvious. If your industry is shrinking, the danger signs for you are especially acute. If your products or services are no longer in demand, eventually you are going to be unemployed unless your company can leapfrog into the next generation of products. This has been accomplished successfully (for example, IBM made the transition from accounting machines to computers), but far more often the task is overpowering and a new generation of companies comes into existence. For example, IBM is now struggling to make the transition from mainframe computing to desktop computing, and has undergone the first layoffs in its history. And its CEO was fired.

Alternatively, your industry may be growing but simultaneously consolidating. The trick here is to be with one of the winners. The automobile business is much bigger today than it was fifty years ago, but that is of little help to the former employees of Studebaker.

In short, industry troubles can represent serious storm warnings. These warnings are especially dangerous if your job is intimately tied to your industry. If you are the world expert at designing iceboxes but know nothing about refrigerators, or you know everything there is to know about rocket propulsion in a world in which expenditures on weapons and aerospace are declining, or you are great at negotiating the sale of cars to consumers at a time when fixed prices for automobiles are coming into vogue, you have an especially big problem on your hands. It is harder to be an engineer or marketeer in a declining industry than it is to be in a more transferable function like finance, human resources, or, in some cases, sales.

Economy Troubles

This is an obvious category, and not one that requires much elaboration. If the economy is in recession, all jobs are in danger; someone once said that a rising tide lifts all ships, and the same is true in reverse. Ask yourself these questions: Do the newspapers say that the economy is in trouble? Are layoffs occurring in a lot of other industries? Are the revenues of your business or the services of your agency dependent on other large organizations that are having financial difficulties themselves? All of these are danger signals for you and those around you.

Personal Dissatisfaction

This may seem like an odd category, but it is a fact that personal unhappiness on the job is a very good predictor of the likelihood of getting fired. Why? Because your own feelings are often a conscious or unconscious reflection of how others feel about you; conversely, negative feelings on your part can have a considerable effect on how those around you feel about you in return.

Let's take an example. Your boss is somewhat dissatisfied with your work. She hasn't yet started giving you poor performance evaluations, but her interactions with you are ever so slightly strained and it is starting to become obvious that all is not as it should be. You may sense this only at an unconscious level, but inevitably it affects your frame of mind. It may make you work harder and become more determined to succeed, but it may also create negative feelings in you. If you begin to detect these negative feelings in yourself, consider it an early warning sign.

Do you look forward to Mondays or to Fridays? Do you relish new assignments or do they seem a burden to be avoided? When your boss calls you in to talk about something, does this engender fear or do you assume it is to be a straightforward work-related conversation? When talking with friends about your work, are you saying positive or negative things? When something bad happens at work, do you care (as you used to) or just ignore it? If the answers to all these questions suggest that you are less than happy at work, consider the possibility that this attitude is being transmitted to those around you at work, and that it will in turn cause them to view you as a negative influence—*or as someone who would be relatively indifferent to being fired.* That is a club to which you do not want to belong; why make it easier for the company to fire you because it can be presumed that you weren't very happy on the job anyway?

This is not to say that you should start worrying about your job just because there are parts of your work you find less than thrilling. Every job has its mundane or unpleasant elements, and the idea that the grass is always greener elsewhere has been disproved for all of us so many times that it is not worth discussing. What we are describing here is a more fundamental unhappiness, a dissatisfaction with almost every element of how you spend your working life. It would be foolish to think that this kind of attitude will not get transmitted to others. Whether it derives from genuine unhappiness with your work or from a conscious or unconscious reading on your part of how you are being perceived by your boss, an awareness of this personal un-happiness can be a precursor to unemployment.

------------------▼------------------

"Today, only about 6% of terminations are prompted by poor performance . . . about 11% of our clients lose their jobs for stated reasons of personal chemistry, though the actual inci-dence may be higher . . . more than 60% of the people who enter our firm's career continuation programs do so as the result of cutbacks, mergers, or reorganizations."

— *William J. Morin and James C. Cabrera,* Parting Company, *1991.*
From Parting Company: How to Survive the Loss of a Job and Find Another. *Copyright © 1991 by Drake Beam Marin, Inc. Reprinted by permission of the publisher.*

------------------▲------------------

Dangerous Job Categories

Working in an especially vulnerable job type represents one of the most difficult problems of all. These jobs fall into three different cat-egories:

1. You will recall from the earlier discussion of industry troubles that if you have a job that is intimately tied to a particular industry, and that industry is in decline, your employment opportunites are also in decline. These tend to be jobs in product design and market-ing, which are highly industry-specific. In some cases, jobs in sales are industry-specific too, though less frequently. Corporate staff functions (such as in the finance, human resources, or legal depart-ments) and other generic jobs (like secretary, retail clerk, or ware-house worker) are in less danger when the issues are ones of a trou-bled industry. All jobs in an industry are in danger when the industry is in decline, but a secretary in a buggy whip company can still play an important role if the company starts making carburetors, whereas the leather curers and the marketing people who understand horse behavior may become totally irrelevant.

2. The second type of vulnerable job category is the staff-ori-ented job, which under certain conditions is safer but which can be very vulnerable for a different reason. The very fact that secretaries and accounting clerks have jobs that are generic, that is, similar in all companies, means that replacing them is relatively easy. Companies are more reluctant to fire people with very narrow expertise, even

when they are marginal performers, simply because people with their particular skills are so hard to find.

I am reminded of a particular individual in a pharmaceutical company who was employed in the research laboratories as an animal handler. He took care of the monkeys, dogs, and cats that were required by law to be used in testing the safety and efficacy of new medicines. This man had relatively little education and spoke little English. He did not have a lot of upward mobility. But he had an absolutely unbelievable ability to work with animals. Chimpanzees who would attack other handlers would turn to melted butter in his presence. Cats who escaped and practically flew around the room to avoid capture would come to him without the slightest hesitation. As you can imagine, this man had one of the safest jobs in the company.

But most of us don't have that kind of expertise. A boss knows that a secretary who isn't performing up to par is relatively easy to replace. The same goes for an hourly paid assembly worker. If you are easy to replace, you are easier to fire.

3. Finally, and unfortunately, there are jobs that are simply perceived as being less important than others. It may not be fair, but people in public relations, human resources, marketing research, and financial analysis are often the first to go when times get tough or expenses have to be cut. (It is especially ironic that the human resources function is so vulnerable, given that human resources professionals are usually the architects of cutbacks for the rest of the company.) It's not that these are not important functions; it's just that the company can go on without them, whereas it cannot go on without people in manufacturing or sales. If you are in one of these expendable job categories, you should be a bit more nervous about your future.

Being Out of the Loop

Sometimes we get the feeling that our contribution is not as important to others as it used to be. When you sense this, you might ask yourself the following questions:

- Have important meetings taken place to which you were not invited?
- Has a boss or a peer who customarily asked your opinion regarding certain matters all of a sudden quit doing so?
- Does your boss go around you to talk to your subordinates, or are your subordinates doing the same in reverse?
- Have there been company social events to which your peers were invited but from which you were left out?

- Do you feel that others are getting the more interesting, chal-
  lenging, and essential job assignments?
- Is it becoming harder to get your boss to make decisions on
  things you propose?
- Has your mentor been fired or pushed aside?

If any of these things is happening, and especially if this is new behavior by the people around you, you have good reason to be nervous. These may be deliberate acts to send you a message (remember,
most companies and bosses find it very hard to give truly critical performance evaluations, so this could be a substitute), or they may be
subtle signals from people who don't even realize they are sending
them. Whether consciously or inadvertently delivered, these kinds of
messages have meaning. Don't ignore them.

Company Philosophy on Employment

Some companies go to great lengths never to fire their employees. For
years, IBM never laid off anyone, and firing occurred only under the
direst of circumstances. Xerox has a very elaborate review process
that involves some of the most senior people in the company whenever someone is to be terminated. At least with certain classes of their
employees, Japanese companies effectively offer employment for life.

By contrast, other employers, often under the flags of "lean and
mean" management, "maintaining flexibility," and "a determination
to deliver profits to our shareholders regardless of the effort required," show not the slightest reluctance to fire and lay off their employees. Oh, they say the right words at such moments and put on
the appropriate sad faces, but the reality is that their view of the unwritten employment contract is a lot different from what you would
like it to be.

There are plenty of signs to help you determine if you are working in one of these "quick to fire" companies. If your company's management buys into any of those slogans just mentioned, you had better beware. But there are other signs to watch for. Has there been a
history of layoffs and rehiring over very short periods of time? Do
you know people who have been fired for seemingly whimsical reasons? Does your company contest every unemployment claim by employees who have left? Is there tolerance for a highly autocratic style
of management? Is there a tightly worded disclaimer in the employee
handbook to the effect that you can be fired at any time for any rea-

son? All these are signals that your job is at higher risk here than it would be in a company inherently committed to its work force.

Danger of Acquisition or Spinoff

A publicly owned company whose performance has been weak and whose stock price is depressed as a result can be a very attractive acquisition candidate. If top management is opposed to the idea of being acquired, it will make dramatic efforts to increase profitability, which in turn drives up the stock price and makes an unfriendly acquisition more expensive and thus less likely.

So how does a company increase its profits? Well, it either has to sell more products or services without increasing costs or it must sell the same number at reduced cost, or it must raise prices without decreasing unit sales proportionately. There are a variety of ways to try and accomplish these profit objectives, but an obvious one is to reduce the number of people employed by the company. In service businesses, the payroll is by far the largest single expense. In manufacturing companies, payroll tends to be an increasing proportion of expenses in these days of commodity-priced raw materials and supplies. It is thus obvious that companies in danger of being acquired are going to look more critically at their human capital, in other words, at your job.

Alternatively, let's say that your company wants to be acquired, or that you work in a division of a larger parent company that has decided to sell off your business. What is the objective of top management in these circumstances? It is to get the highest price possible for the business. And how can they accomplish this? By increasing profits, of course.

It is very common for companies to cut back on nonessential spending and, in some cases, even on spending that is essential for the long-term health of the enterprise for the sole purpose of "dressing up the books" so that they will look as healthy as possible. They know that the buyers of companies are sophisticated, but anyone would rather buy a healthy business. Furthermore, one of the key justifications for a merger or acquisition is that fewer people will be required to run the combined businesses than are required to run them separately. Duplicate functions or duplicate locations can be eliminated at a considerable savings. If you are in a company going through this kind of thought process, whether for defensive or positive reasons, you must assume that your job risk has increased.

Arrival of New Management

You may have a new boss. Your division or company may have a new president. You may have been acquired. Or for some reason, the key decision makers have new faces or names.

It doesn't take a brain surgeon to know that this kind of change could be dangerous. It could also be positive; if your company is struggling, new management at the top may be exactly what is needed, and your prospects may improve dramatically. On the other hand, new management brings new ideas. These ideas could include hiring people they already know and trust for key jobs, and these people in turn will hire some people they know and trust, and so on until it gets to your level. Alternatively, new management may be less committed to your business, or your department, or your particular function than the previous management was. In any event, the arrival of new management is a wake-up call, and you must listen to the alarm.

The Storm Warning Game

These were ten very clear danger signals that you can detect if you are paying attention. Now you should play the Storm Warning Game.

Assign each of these danger signals a possible ten points. If, on examination, the danger signal is totally invisible, give it ten points. For example, if your performance evaluations are stellar, and you know you are held in higher regard by your boss and the other key decision makers than are your peers, you get ten points on that one. Likewise, if your industry is growing rapidly, and everything you read and hear suggests that you work in an industry that is relatively small and expected to get very large (for example, wireless communications or organic foods), give yourself ten points on that one as well. Conversely, if a particular category hits you between the eyes as an obvious problem, you get a zero for that category. Maybe your company is steadily losing market share to two of its competitors. Or your division is in the process of being acquired. You see how it works.

If you feel that a particular category is too hard to call, which certainly will be the case in many situations, give it an intermediate grade. It isn't useful to be unnecessarily precise about this; the exercise will work fine if you assign each category one of three grades: ten, five, or zero.

Add up the scores. If you get 100 points, you are either the luckiest person on earth or totally blind. In the real world, no one gets 100 points. Go back and take the test again.

If your score is 80 to 99 *and there are no zeros in the individual categories,* this probably is about as good as things get. But the qualifier is very important. No matter how good things are in your company, your industry, and the economy, you are going to get fired sooner or later if your performance evaluations are terrible. And no matter how strong your performance is, your job is at risk if your company is in the process of being sold. So you get membership in this group only if none of the danger signals have waving red flags attached to them.

If your score is 50 to 79, you have a lot of company. Even if there are no individual zeros in the scoring, you have to be on the lookout. There are forces at work here that put you at risk, and the fact that there are enough of them means that there are several ways you could lose your job. Keep your eyes peeled.

If your score is 49 or lower, you have serious problems on your hands. Write yourself a résumé and buy one of the books that can help you learn how to examine new career opportunities.

Chapter 2

Preparing for the Worst

So you've played the Storm Warning Game, and the news isn't good. Somewhere deep down you feel there's a danger that you are going to lose your job. It may not be today, it may not be this week or even this month, but the warning bells are starting to ring. What should you do?

Although it will cost you a little money, it might not be a bad idea to arrange a consultation with an experienced employment attorney (see Chapter 9). This probably will cost you between $100 and $250. He or she will be able to give you good advice as to how to prepare yourself. If the warning bells are ringing loudly, this is what I would suggest you do first. Whether you do it or not, however, there are several other very specific steps you should take. And you should take them now. None costs any money. None puts you at any real risk. None takes very much time. But all of them will help protect you if that unwelcome day arrives.

Crucial Steps to Take to Protect Yourself

1. Look at Your Personnel File

In some regards, the most important step is the riskiest. You want to look at your personnel file. This may be the easiest request in the world or a very complicated one, depending on the state where you live. Look up your state in Appendix I at the end of this book for a synopsis of the laws in your state on reviewing these files. In a substantial number of states you have a clear legal right to review your file, typically after providing a written request. Also, read the section on personnel file access in Chapter 5.

Ideally, you will already have established a pattern of reviewing your file on a regular basis. If you live in a state that allows for such review, and most states do, I suggest that every six or twelve months you ask to look at your file. You might find something of value, and it will establish a pattern so that it will not seem unusual when you come back and ask to see the file again.

In states where there is no law, most employers will let you look at your file or have a copy of it without much trouble. In some cases they will not. In almost all cases, regardless of the law, someone is likely to ask you why you want to see the file, especially if you are asking for the first time. This obviously is none of their business, but you are trying to make the least noise possible in this process; you don't want to send a signal to your employer that something is amiss.

You should tailor a story to fit your company and your circumstances. For instance, if your company has a policy of written performance evaluations and you typically get a copy of yours at evaluation time, just say that you have misplaced your past copies and want to get new ones. You can say that you are applying for a loan and the bank wants your history of salary increases (if these are not in your file, and they often are not, be sure to make a separate request for them from the payroll department). You can say that you are writing your will and that your lawyer wants to make sure he understands your salary history, pension entitlements, and other benefits. Or you can just say that you read an article that says you should always have a current copy of your personnel records.

Obviously you should *not* say that you are concerned about being fired and want a copy of your file for protection.

If your company refuses to give you access to the file, and you live in a state where it can legally deny you access, drop the subject and save this fight for another day.

Why do you want these records? First of all, you really do want to review all your past performance evaluations. Good evaluations won't prevent you from getting fired, but it is wise to review your recollection of the facts and very useful in your termination interview to know what the records say; termination interviews are discussed in detail in Chapter 3.

Second, if you do get fired and there is litigation later (see all of Chapters 9 and 10), you will want to have (or to have seen) the same documents that your company will have in court. Getting them while you are still employed is typically a lot easier than getting them later.

Finally, you may learn something new. Lots of companies put information in personnel records without mentioning it to you at the time, for instance, notes from supervisors independent of the formal performance evaluation process, medical records, and documentation of awards received. Some of this may be new information to you; more likely, the information will simply provide a fuller and better picture of how a dispassionate third party would regard you if he or she had access to your files.

Obtaining access to these files does entail a level of risk. In spite of the laws, some companies view these requests with suspicion, and human resources departments sometimes report such requests back to the managers involved. The better the law in your state, and the bigger and more sophisticated your employer, the less likely it is that there will be any problem. Under all circumstances, however, you should have an explanation in mind and should make the request in a nonconfrontational way.

2. Locate Whatever Materials Bear on Your Employment

Gather in one place the original copies of any performance evaluations you have on hand, especially if you do not obtain access to your personnel file. (In some states, performance reviews are kept separate from other personnel matters, and the courts have upheld employer requests that employees not be given access to these reviews even though access to other personnel records is allowed.)

Your collection effort should also include past medical records (most likely from your health insurance files, which may also be available from your doctor or health insurer), records of work missed because of illness, information on vacations taken (so that you can determine if any vacation time has accrued), letters or documents congratulating you for work well done, reports you have received on accumulations in pension and profit sharing accounts, at least five years' worth of W2 forms, and at least five years' worth of salary increase and bonus information. Gather anything you can imagine needing if you were going to try and make a case to a judge that you were considered a good and loyal employee.

3. Obtain a Copy of the Employee Handbook

Both the current handbook and older editions may prove useful. You may have a copy of the one you were given when you were hired, and your company library (if there is one) may have old copies as well.

This probably seems like an odd suggestion, but employee handbooks often represent the only written document that can be construed as an employment contract. There have been lawsuits in which relatively innocuous wording in the handbook (for example, "we are a company with low turnover and great loyalty to our employees, and pride ourselves on continually retraining our employees so that the skills of our work force never become obsolete") has been sufficient to trigger a claim of guaranteed lifetime employment. Companies are becoming much more sophisticated at wording these documents, but having them in hand will help you analyze one source of "promises" that the company has made to you regarding employment. The employee handbook also serves as the best single summary of benefits and employment practices available, and this will help you implement step 2.

Be especially thorough in looking for disclaimers in the handbook, for example, statements that the handbook specifically does not constitute an employment contract, or that all employees are "at-will" employees. These disclaimers could be crucial to your ability to negotiate with your employer or to file a lawsuit.

You should also find out if your employer issues a supervisor's manual of some kind. As companies grow more sophisticated, it is more common for them to distribute documents to supervisors to help them avoid sexual harassment and wrongful discipline and discharge situations. If you are a supervisor, you would have received one of these. You should look for the company's guidelines on termination as well as for any inconsistencies with the employee handbook. For example, the employee handbook may say that you can be fired at any time for any reason, but the supervisory handbook may give a number of examples where firing is inappropriate or illegal. These kinds of inconsistencies could help you later in negotiations or in a lawsuit.

4. Start to Keep a Daily Record of Everything Consequential That Happens to You on the Job

If your boss commends you on a piece of work, write down the date and details. Be sure to include the names of witnesses, if any. If you have a performance review, even if you receive a copy in writing, go back to your work site immediately and write down whatever your boss said while reviewing you in person. A lot of the words exchanged in this process may explain, augment, or even contradict those written on paper, and you want to make sure you have a record of these. Treat nothing as trivial; even an offhand comment about your work, your vacation rights, your co-workers, or some vague allusion to future projects or responsibilities could prove invaluable if you and your employer should find yourselves in conflict.

Keep in mind that these notes are "discoverable" in the case of a lawsuit; that is, you may be required to divulge their existence and contents. For this reason, be especially careful to keep them factual. Do not write down negative comments about your boss, your own feelings, or anyone's personality. Restrict yourself to a simple chronicle of events and of who said what to whom.

A practice that has become increasingly common is for employees to tape-record these conversations secretly. The argument for this is obvious: It gives you an exact record of what was said, both for your own recollection and for a judge or jury should there be litigation.

This is a high-risk strategy, however. First of all, if you live in a state that requires both parties to consent to the taping of a conversation, you are breaking the law. Second, if you are discovered in the process or at any time while still employed by that company, you can be sure that this behavior will be viewed as a sign of disloyalty. Third, even if the tape supports your argument in front of a jury, legal experts say that there is some tendency for juries to view surreptitious taping as sneaky even in states where it is legal. Finally, the content of the tape itself could work against you; keep in mind that your words will be recorded too, and you may say something that compromises your position.

In general, I recommend against adopting this practice. I would use it only in extreme cases, for example, with a boss who has a history of saying one thing to your face and something else behind your back. It can also be a good idea in sexual harassment situations, as these are ones in which the boss almost always denies having engaged in such behavior. But even in these circumstances, I would suggest that you consult an attorney before proceeding.

5. Read the Termination Laws Applicable in Your State, Found in Appendix I

Federal law (detailed in Chapter 11) often is useless to you unless some form of illegal discrimination has taken place. Individual states, however, have laws covering a wide variety of topics, including when you must receive your final paycheck, whether or not you are owed an explanation if you are terminated, and the circumstances under which you may not be terminated. You should familiarize yourself with these in a general way and be prepared to learn them in much more detail quickly if your employment situation deteriorates.

6. Obtain Information as to How Company Employees Were Treated During Previous Layoffs

This includes regular layoffs (both permanent and temporary), special early retirement programs, and outright firings. If your employer has had a formal layoff, this information should be quite easy to gather. Information on fired individuals is more difficult to come by, and probably available only from the individuals themselves. If you have fired people, you have some sense of your company's policies and level of generosity with regard to severance and benefits, but it is worth gathering whatever information you can.

As with looking at your personnel file, this kind of information gathering should be conducted with delicacy. Too many questions and someone (like your boss) may start wondering why you are asking such questions. If you are a supervisor, an obvious reason is to get some guidelines about how to fire one of your own people; in fact, you may be able to go right to the human resources department for help. Perhaps you have a good friend who was fired or laid off who would not mind sharing with you the details of his or her treatment. There may be newspaper articles about layoffs in your community if they were of any size. Regardless of how you gather the information, what you are looking for is some sense of precedent with regard to how fired people (or those who have been encouraged to quit via early retirement programs) have been treated.

7. Read Very, Very Carefully the Sections of Chapter 3 That Discuss How to Behave When You Get Fired

If you get nothing else out of this book, I want you to remember that your behavior in those few minutes when you get the bad news could have a profound effect on your life. *Be sure you understand that under no circumstances whatsoever should you sign anything in your initial termination meeting.*

8. Start Preparing a Résumé

This is not very time-consuming, and it is a good exercise for any person serious about his or her career. The reason to do this is not the obvious one of having a résumé available in case you are fired, though that is a pretty good one. The more important objective is to force yourself to do an in-depth review and evaluation of your career path to date. Are there experiences you are missing? Maybe this is

the right time to try and get them. Do you know how to reach all your
former bosses for references? Listing all your past roles will help you
think of who they are so that you can track them down. Does the
story of your past job changes or transfers hold together? This is the
chance to think about such subjects in an atmosphere not emotionally
charged by the trauma of unemployment.

What You Should Not Do

No matter how sure you are that the axe is coming, no matter how
unhappy you are on the job, no matter what extenuating circumstances you can convince yourself apply to your situation, *do not under
any circumstances take home any materials, information, or supplies that
belong to your employer.* The fact that you worked on a project does not
make it your property. The fact that you have a customer list for the
sales territory does not make them your customers or entitle you to a
copy of that list. The fact that you work for a company does not entitle
you to take its staplers and dictionaries.

Keep in mind that your attorney will probably be forced to divulge the fact that you have such information in your possession if
asked by your former employer. Also keep in mind how this "theft"
(which is what your ex-employer will call it) will look to your new
employer.

Obviously, certain materials are yours, like the employee handbook or copies of your performance evaluations. I am not suggesting
that you must leave your own possessions at the office. But you
should be very careful in defining what is yours.

This may seem obvious, but the issues are serious ones. We are a
highly litigious society. The judicial process has been quite sympathetic in recent years to employees who have been wronged, but it
also has been quite sympathetic to employers whose trade secrets
have been stolen. In some cases, these are criminal offenses, especially if technical information is involved.

Furthermore, any employer who would find you more attractive
because you had such confidential materials in your possession is not
an employer you would want to work for. Groucho Marx is reputed
to have said that he would not join any club that would take him as a
member; you shouldn't join any employer who is hiring you in the
hopes of gaining secrets that rightfully belong to your former employer.

Should I Beat Them to the Punch?

This is one of the most difficult questions for the person whose job is in jeopardy. The handwriting is on the wall. Or you have a suspicion that someone is getting ready to put it up there. The company has troubles. You have a new boss. You are unhappy, or someone is unhappy with you. For whatever reason, you are feeling vulnerable to losing your job. Should you quit? You have several alternatives:

1. Do nothing and hope for the best.
2. Make an active effort to save your job when you think you are in trouble.
3. Quit.
4. Quit with help from your boss or the company.
5. Stay on the job but start looking for a new employer at the same time.

Let's examine each of these in turn.

1. Do Nothing

The good news about this alternative is that it is easy. It takes no time, no energy, and no money. You do nothing proactively that could get you into trouble. In short, you could behave like an ostrich.

Sometimes this is exactly the right thing to do, but rarely. If you are feeling vulnerable in your employment, at a minimum you should take the eight steps outlined earlier. You should gather the intellectual resources necessary to prepare yourself in case you get fired. You should examine your finances and decide if you want to start changing your spending habits. It is the underlying thesis of this book that you should always be "ready to be fired." Unless you own the company or in some other way feel bulletproof, doing nothing is unacceptable.

2. Try to Fix the Situation

The question of whether a job situation is worth trying to save is a very complicated one. Usually by the time you figure out that your job is in danger, there is little you can do. But it depends a lot on the circumstances. If you have basic personality problems with your boss, these are *very* unlikely to be resolved, and the only logical alternative is to try to transfer to another department. If you like your employer in most other ways, this is worth a try.

If the problems relate to your company or industry, there is little you can do anyway.

If the problem is that you are failing in some specific way to meet the expectations of your boss, one school of thought is that you ought to talk openly with your boss about this, recognize that there is a problem, dedicate yourself to solving it, and work out a plan with your boss for doing so. This can work well when the problems are ones that can be solved, for example, problems of time management, of work output, of specific skills deficiencies, or anything else that in theory can be improved by effort and training.

The danger, of course, is that when you initiate conversations with your boss, you give him or her the opportunity to take the occasion to tell you how really terribly you are performing and to start the termination process in an unofficial way. However, if you see bad news coming on the horizon anyway, and if you have prepared yourself by reading this book, the risks are relatively minimal. Remember, this is a conversation you want to initiate only if you really want to save your job and think you have some chance of doing so.

3. Quit

This obviously is the most drastic step you can take. When is it appropriate? When circumstances are so terrible that you cannot stand it there another day longer. When your work is adversely affecting your health, your family life, and your emotional well-being. In short, when continued employment is intolerable.

What is wrong with quitting? The simple answer is that the best vantage point for finding a new job is while you still have the old one. This simply is the psychology of the hiring process. People who are unemployed are perceived to be in that state for one of several reasons: They got fired for some substantive reason; they got laid off along with a bunch of others who were not considered the "keepers"; they quit to beat their bosses to the punch; they were so unhappy that they couldn't stand working there another day; or they quit for some positive reason (for example, "I wanted to work in California and there simply was no way to job hunt in California while I was living in Pennsylvania"; "I inherited a little money and wanted to take a few months off for the first time in my life"; "I don't like lying to my employer and felt that looking for a job while I worked for them was the same as lying").

In one way or another, all these reasons are either clearly negative or open to negative interpretations, and they are usually so interpreted. Unemployed people, no matter how tidy their explanations and how impressive their track records, are suspect. Any expert on interviewing and reference checking will tell you that most unemployed people in fact have in some way or another been pushed out of their jobs or have figured out that this was going to happen to them.

Furthermore, the legal experts say that you are seriously compromising any chances of a lawsuit if you decide to quit. In fact, one renowned employment attorney told me that he simply won't take cases where the person quit before filing suit.

Yes, I have met people who genuinely quit for reasons of principle. And I have met lots of people who have been fired for reasons that reflect far more poorly on their former employers than on them as individuals. But quitting always raises a red flag. And the job-hunting process is tough enough without carrying around an extra millstone.

Perhaps most important, people who quit before finding a new job don't take much with them. Quitters usually don't get severance pay (but see No. 4 below). They usually don't get health insurance. They typically do not qualify for unemployment compensation (see the more detailed discussion of this in Chapter 5). In short, they usually get nothing. On top of this, they may be viewed as traitors, or at a minimum leave their bosses in the lurch for a brief period, which can have a negative effect on references.

My advice? Don't quit except in the most dire circumstances, and consult an employment attorney before doing so. The advantages you gain are far more than offset by the leverage and benefits you lose.

There is a special category of quitting known in the courts as a "constructive discharge." This is a situation in which you quit to escape illegal or intolerable employment practices or conditions. In general, you would have to prove that the situation was so intolerable that any reasonable person would have felt forced to resign, and you must have given your employer a chance to rectify the situation. If these circumstances apply, the courts may treat you as a fired employee entitled to whatever pay and benefits other such employees receive. However, you will have to use the courts to get this money, and constructive discharge is very hard to prove. The most common situations in which it has been provable are in cases of sexual harassment or harassment against members of a protected minority group.

4. Negotiate Leaving the Company

This is a somewhat more attractive variant of No. 3, but it has its own set of perils. There are times when a negotiated departure can make sense for both parties. Let's say it becomes obvious to you that there are going to have to be some cutbacks, and you figure that you may well be part of them. Furthermore, you have a good relationship with your boss. You know that if you leave suddenly he will be in a short-term pickle because it will be hard to fill in for you.

Under these circumstances, it might make sense to go to him with a message like the following: "Bob, you and I both know that there are going to have to be some cutbacks. For that and a lot of other reasons, I have been giving thought to leaving. I don't want to mess up your operations, but at the same time I need to be thinking about the future. An idea that occurs to me is that with your approval, I could start looking for a new job, but with the understanding that I will continue doing my current job and help you train a replacement. I will need to take some time for the job-hunting process, but I will hold up my end at work. In turn, I want to be sure that I will have your continued support and that I won't be left swinging in the wind if the layoffs arrive."

This kind of approach works best when you work for a generally supportive company, have a good relationship with your boss, and have done well on the job. Your boss is spared having to think about firing you for reasons beyond his control, and is also assured of an orderly transition. You get a continued flow of income without having to worry about having your job search uncovered. If your boss is determined to keep you, he gets a chance to talk you into staying without artificial time pressures. And you may be spared in the cutback process because your boss knows of your plans, which will allow you to continue job hunting from a base of being employed, and enable you to tell the world truthfully that you are leaving voluntarily rather than being pushed out.

The risk, of course, is that your boss won't go along with this scenario. At best, you have now compromised your relationship with him. At worst, he views the idea as evidence of your lack of allegiance, and hastens the process of getting you out the door. *If you take this approach, you must be psychologically and financially prepared for the possibility that it could backfire.* But when it works, it can be the ideal solution.

5. Don't Quit but Quietly Start Looking for a New Job

This is the most common solution, and usually the right one. You continue to bring in a salary, you continue to avoid the stigma of being unemployed, and if the layoffs come you can still anticipate some incremental salary and benefits.

The problem, of course, is that job hunting is time-consuming, and you must be very careful to balance the search process with the need to maintain your level of performance at work. Also, some companies will fire you summarily if they hear you are talking with others about a job, in which case you lose out on whatever salary continuation and benefits you might normally have received. Nevertheless, this usually is the right decision. Notwithstanding whatever stories you have heard to the contrary, very few people have been fired when their job search was uncovered, and most job searches stay confidential until you go in to resign. These risks are generally lower than those inherent in the other alternatives discussed.

Chapter 3

The Termination Interview

Here you are. The boss has called you in. You've done everything you could to prepare for the possibility of termination. You have gathered facts and steeled yourself psychologically. But the moment is at hand, and your anxiety is at a peak.

In a perfect world, all bosses would be sympathetic and enlightened. You would agree that things had not worked out or that, for some reason, it was time to move on to bigger and better things. Your conversation would be short, friendly, free of criticism and recriminations. Your boss would take a factual approach, without argument, attack, or apologies. You would reciprocate.

This fantasy is actually realized from time to time, but not very often. These situations are inherently full of conflicting emotions, made worse by the overlay of personalities and financial issues. They are difficult in the best of circumstances. As a result, a few rules of the road are necessary. Here are six:

1. *Whatever you do, no matter how greatly you feel provoked, don't lose your temper.* You may have good reason to blow your stack, throw something at your boss, and insult his wife and children. The way you have been treated may be grossly unfair. But now is the time to take the long-term view. You are about to negotiate for severance; anything that irritates your boss is going to make that negotiation harder. Furthermore, you are dependent on this person for references that will help you land your next job. There simply is no percentage in making him feel that you have acted unprofessionally—or in proving to him yet further that firing you was a good idea.

2. *Use your psychological advantage.* Strange though it may seem, at this moment you have maximum psychological leverage. Firing

28

someone is the most stressful experience a boss can go through. If you are being released as part of a large layoff, your boss probably has relatively fixed guidelines and therefore feels less stress, but still it is painful. If yours is an individual termination, he may be just as upset as you are, and may experience many of the same emotions. Think about this as the negotiations start, because it is your single most powerful weapon.

▼

"Keep in mind that having to fire someone is an extremely stressful assignment even for the most experienced managers. What's more, companies usually want dismissed employees to be out of their building and away from the remaining employees as quickly as possible to prevent vengeful sabotage or spreading anti-company sentiment. Therefore, a person being fired exercises a substantial amount of negotiating power."

—Your Rights in the Workplace, *by Dan Lacey and Nolo Press, 1991.*

▲

3. *Don't start your negotiations now.* Your boss will press you on this point, because this is an open wound and the company wants it closed as soon as possible. But it is not in your self-interest to finalize anything this quickly.

After you listen to what your boss has to say, which may include specifics as to the severance package the company is offering, you should reply as follows: "Needless to say, this comes as a big shock. I was not planning to lose my job, and doing so has many ramifications for me. Obviously I have a lot to think about. Let's make an appointment to get together tomorrow afternoon [or Monday afternoon if this conversation is taking place on a Friday] so we can discuss what you have said in more depth." This message should be delivered calmly, which may take a heroic effort on your part. This is the time to be at your most professional. The fact that every fiber in your body is telling you to strangle the person in front of you is totally understandable, but save your energy and passion for more important things to come.

4. *Sign nothing.* Especially do not sign anything implying that you agree with your severance package or that you promise not to sue the company. If the company gives you anything in writing, take it along and show it to a lawyer or some other knowledgeable person, but do not sign it.

There are isolated circumstances in which companies involved in hostile takeovers come storming in and demand that everyone sign a non-compete agreement or a severance agreement on a moment's notice, with the threat that employees will lose all severance privileges if they refuse to sign. This is totally unethical, and the company runs the serious risk of a class action suit (brought by many people simultaneously), which they would fear even more than a wrongful discharge suit from an individual. Many attorneys would advise you to sign nothing in such circumstances and to take your chances later, but this is a call that only you can make. Fortunately, it is a reasonably rare event and not usually associated with common garden-variety terminations.

There are other circumstances in which you will be offered the chance to resign rather than be fired. This may make sense, but again, do not agree to it now.

5. *Gather your wits as best you can and start taking notes.* It will be hard to concentrate given what is taking place, but concentrate you must. There are several reasons for writing everything down. First, because it is an emotional situation, it will be hard to remember the details later unless you do. You want to make sure that you know (and can document in court if necessary) what you were told about why you were being fired and what the company is offering you. Don't try to give elaborate responses at this point; just write your notes and ask for clarification if necessary.

Second, it is a great negotiating technique. It forces your boss (or whoever is doing the firing) to be especially careful with words, and in some cases more complimentary or conciliatory than might otherwise be the case. Everyone knows that critical words on paper sound a lot worse than when they are delivered orally, and no one wants to be portrayed as having been overly negative or critical.

Finally, taking notes marks you as a serious person. This might sound odd at first blush, but what you want to convey is that you are not just going to roll over and play dead. By taking notes, you signal that you are going to go off and think hard about the topic at hand and perhaps discuss it with others (like a lawyer, although you don't want to mention lawyers).

As discussed in Chapter 2, I am not generally in favor of tape-recording conversations secretly. In this case, however, some people bring a tape recorder openly to the meeting and ask for (or don't bother to ask for) permission to tape. My instincts are that this will cause your boss to become so cautious that some of the things you would like him to say won't get said. I prefer note taking as a less threatening but almost as effective a strategy.

6. *Don't plead for your job unless your financial circumstances are so desperate that you feel you must.* This rarely works and only makes you seem weaker in the eyes of management. Even if you convince them to let you stay, your renewed lease on life with the company almost certainly will be temporary, and their image of you will be forever tainted by having seen you beg. If the pleading doesn't work, as it most likely won't, you will only feel worse after effectively having been fired twice. This will also affect the references they give you. I cannot remember a single instance of someone who got his firing reversed and then went on to a happy and successful career within the same organization.

Before your meeting the next day, you should gather whatever information you can. Are other people being fired at the same time? Find out from them, if you can, what they are being offered. Do you have an attorney? Contact him or her for advice. (However, the next-door neighbor who happens to be an attorney and who helped you on a real estate closing isn't going to know the subtleties of employment law, which is changing rapidly; for this, be sure you find an expert.) Do a quick analysis again of your financial situation. Read Chapter 4 in detail so that you know the guidelines for severance. Prepare yourself to make a positive and knowledgeable presentation.

Now a few more words on the psychology of negotiation. As stated earlier, you are in the odd position of being the person fired and yet negotiating with someone who is feeling great guilt. Unless you are being fired for some dastardly deed like stealing from the company, in which case you should be happy the police are not in the room, your boss is very uncomfortable with the situation. After all, at some level your boss too has failed, whether in the hiring process, the training process, or the motivation process, or you would not find yourselves in this pickle. And I stress that both of you are in the pickle, which is your negotiating leverage.

Your boss also has other worries. There may be legal issues to confront, relating to discrimination or to a variety of other considerations; these are covered in Chapter 11 and Appendix I. He has to worry about the effect of your firing on the remaining employees who will be highly attuned to your treatment and whether it is fair or not. He has a boss who does not want to see a fuss made. He must worry about the image of the company in the employment marketplace, and the fact that you may go out and disparage him and the company in many ways. And your boss probably feels genuine guilt at intruding in such a negative way in another person's life.

The key to negotiating success is to enter the conversations with a businesslike, positive attitude. As soon as your boss sees that you are there to negotiate rather than to argue, the process will get dramatically easier. In fact, you should say at the very outset that you realize his decision is final, that you have thought about the situation and your financial needs, and that you are prepared to work out an agreement.

Some companies are using the human resources department to deliver the message that you are being fired. The bad news is that the human resources person delivering the message feels less guilt, and so is more difficult to negotiate with. The good news is that the human resources department understands keenly the legal vulnerability of the company, and thus may be more concerned to avoid lawsuits. On balance, however, if you have to be fired, you are better off if the message comes from your boss and any negotiations are with him.

Part Two

The Negotiation

Chapter 4

Keeping What You Have

Companies vary greatly in their termination practices. Large companies tend to have written severance and termination policies. In fact, one study by Right Associates shows that 79 percent of companies with more than 5,000 employees have such policies, as compared with 47 percent of companies with fewer than 500 employees. As a result, large companies are less flexible in what they are willing to negotiate. On the other hand, they tend to be more acutely aware of the legal issues and may be more accommodating if they sense that they are in a gray area of the law. Overall, experience suggests that smaller companies are the most likely to structure individual severance packages.

Another critical issue is whether you are part of a mass layoff or are being terminated individually. In the former case, there is very little flexibility unless you can somehow differentiate yourself from the group, such as by age. Most of the opportunities for this differentiation lie with the legal alternatives discussed in Chapter 11. If you are being fired individually, the chances for negotiation are greater.

Keep in mind that what you are after is a severance *package*. This may be the most important fact of your negotiations. Severance is not just salary continuation. In fact, the continued payment of your salary may be far less important than continuation of your company-paid health insurance, vesting of your stock options, or some other factor. Do not be misled into thinking that salary should be your primary focus, though it certainly should be an important one.

Finally, keep in mind that with certain exceptions, like federally mandated health insurance continuation under the Consolidated Omnibus Budget Reconciliation Act (COBRA), *no company is required to pay you any severance* unless it has a severance policy in place, and there is no legal requirement that there be such a policy. The com-

pany may have backed itself into a corner with written or oral severance policies or with precedents in the payment of severance to others, but in the absence of such policies there is no law anywhere but
in a few isolated states preventing an employer from firing you with
no severance pay whatsoever. Fortunately, most employers ignore
this power and pay severance in most circumstances.

In this chapter, I want to examine compensation and benefits elements that you have already enjoyed as an employee and that you
wish to have continued for as long as possible during the termination
process.

Salary Continuation

As a simple rule of thumb, most companies calculate severance on
the basis of one or two weeks of salary for each year of employment.
Thus, if you have been employed at the company for twelve years,
you typically would get not less than twelve nor more than twenty-
four weeks of salary in the form of severance pay.

However, this varies dramatically. It is affected by the size of the
company, by the level of the employee (executives get more than administrative and technical employees), by the employee's length of
service, by employment contracts, and by a lot of other factors. For
example, the age of the employee is often taken into consideration,
as is the ability of the employee to start collecting from the retirement
plan, if there is one. The definitive survey on this topic was conducted
by Right Associates in 1991 and is shown in Figure 1.

As you can see, the more senior the employee's position is, the
more generous the treatment will be when it comes to severance.
Only 19 percent of key executives fall within the one to two weeks per
year of service guideline, whereas 49 percent of administrative and
technical personnel are in this category. Furthermore, when companies set limits, they set them higher for key executives. Payments of
one to three years of salary continuation are not unusual at high executive levels, but they are very rare down in the ranks.

These practices are not as discriminatory in favor of highly paid
employees as they sound. In general, the more highly paid the employee is, the longer it takes to land a new job; people earning over
$100,000 per year often require a six-to twelve-month job search, and
are more likely to have to relocate. More senior employees are also
more subject to losing their jobs for somewhat capricious reasons: A
new president is hired and wants to hire his old friend as the vice

Figure 1. Type of salary continuation by employee function.

	Key Executive	Manager	Supervisor	Administrative/ Technical
1 week's pay per year of service	13%	31%	36%	36%
2 weeks' pay per year of service	6%	13%	13%	13%
3 weeks' pay per year of service	2%	2%	2%	1%
1 month's pay per year of service	6%	7%	5%	4%
A multiple of annual salary	7%	3%	2%	1%
A percentage of annual salary	8%	6%	4%	3%
Employment agreement	24%	5%	2%	2%
No set formula	31%	17%	14%	13%
Other	14%	18%	17%	16%

SOURCE: *Severance: The Corporate Response* (Right Associates, 1991).
Note: Some companies use multiple formulas, so totals may not add up to 100%.

president of sales, so the current vice president of sales is out. Companies recognize the no-fault aspects of such firings and accordingly are more generous.

For your specific purposes, you obviously must know if your company has a formal severance policy. This was information you should have gathered as a result of reading Chapter 2, whether from the company handbook or from past severance practices you were able to uncover. Negotiating your particular salary continuation should be based on any such information you have gathered and on whatever specific case you can make for yourself; remember that you are after a package, not just a salary.

The time span of salary continuation is not the only salary-related issue. You must consider whether you want to negotiate to take your severance pay in a lump sum or have it extended over time. Companies are split about evenly in this area, and the arguments on each side are quite straightforward.

The lump sum gets you your money in advance and avoids any question of having a stream of payments cut off if you take a new job. You can invest any part of the lump sum that you do not need for living expenses. On the other hand, a lump sum may create an unusually large tax obligation in the year it is received, and many companies use the lump sum as a mechanism to get you off the payroll, out of their hair, and out of any benefit programs (like health insurance or pension vesting) that are dependent on your existence as an employee "on the payroll." You must also worry about how to invest a lump sum at a time when you have more important issues on your mind, and there is a tendency to make poor investment decisions and to waste valuable time on them under these circumstances.

A payout of your severance salary over time typically maintains your participation in benefit programs. It spreads out the tax obligation and for some people makes financial planning more orderly. You continue to feel somewhat like an employee even though you aren't going to work, and this is a psychological benefit that should not be minimized. On the other hand, it creates the need to negotiate on an additional issue: What happens if you take a new position? About two-thirds of companies insist on a provision in the severance agreement stipulating that severance payments will stop if you take a new job.

Your company may have fixed rules that control how its salary severance payments are made. If the rules are flexible, the right answer depends a lot on your psychology, your financial health, and the company's, and your perception of your job prospects. If your employer is on shaky ground financially, that is a powerful argument in favor of settling for a lump sum. If you think that another job is just around the corner, a lump sum settlement is attractive in this case too.

But if your employer is healthy and your job prospects uncertain, payments over time are preferable, if for no other reason than it leaves open the possibility of reopening severance conversations if time is running out and you still have no new employment. It is a surprise to many people to learn that many companies have an unwritten policy of adding some time to the severance agreement in situations where the fired employee is in some financial distress. Human resources executives prefer not to talk about such practices, but they are reasonably common. Keep in mind, however, that there is no way to force such an extension, and you may have signed a document upon departure saying that you understand that the severance you are getting is all you will receive under any circumstances. In spite of this, I prefer severance payments over time in most cases.

On the issue of cutting off severance payments if the ex-employee accepts a new job, companies are becoming more enlightened. They have figured out that absolute payment cutoffs associated with accepting new employment have a tendency to motivate some people to start a new job on the last possible day before severance pay runs out, thus maximizing the payout by their ex-employer. As a result, a hybrid formula is coming into favor whereby you get a portion of your remaining severance pay if you accept a position before the severance term ends. Thus, for example, an ex-employee with a twelve-month severance package who accepts a new position after six months may get an additional three months of severance, for a total of nine months of pay. The fired employee receives more money in aggregate when his severance pay is added to his new salary, and the firing company spends less than might have been necessary.

With regard to this and all other sections in this chapter, remember that you may have legal leverage that affects your negotiating strength. This is discussed in great detail in chapters 9, 10, and 11 and in Appendix I. In general, if you are over age 40, disabled, or a member of a minority group, or if you are female, you are more likely to have some legal leverage. Keep this in mind throughout the negotiating process; you can be sure that your soon-to-be ex-employer is thinking about it.

There are other issues regarding salary continuation that are also worth considering. For instance, if your employer is on shaky financial ground, try to get the company to escrow your future salary severance payments if you are not being paid in a lump sum (that is, the company pays a lump sum into an escrow account at a bank and the funds are disbursed to you on the regular payroll schedule). Also, negotiate for a clause stipulating that each salary payment is to be paid on a specific date and listing interest and/or penalties to be paid if that date is missed. Finally, be sure to take into account any interrupted service you may have. If you worked for the company for five years, left for two years, then returned for another five years, you certainly want to negotiate for treatment as a ten-year employee when the severance calculations are made.

▼

"It's been clear for years, after all, that in the world of huge corporations there's nothing more lucrative than being fired well."

—*Calvin Trillin in "Corporate Triumphs," King Features Syndicate, September 28, 1986. Reprinted with special permission of King Features Syndicate.*

▲

Bonus Plans and Other Regular Cash Compensation

Bonus plans often constitute the stickiest situations in severance negotiations. There are several reasons for this. First, many bonus plans
are discretionary, often at the whim of one individual, so there is no
formula for making a calculation as to what is "due" an employee at
any particular point in time.

Second, even those plans that are formula-based do not lend
themselves to simple calculations. If the formula is based on a performance review measurement multiplied by a fixed pool of money,
there can be debate about the performance evaluation (especially
when you are being fired). If the formula is based on a pool whose
size is determined by the financial performance of the company, the
size of this pool is usually calculated just once a year, which probably
will not coincide with the firing. If the formula is based on the attain-
ment of specific results (for example, sales quotas or manufacturing
output), there is likewise the issue of when these results are mea-
sured. In the case of sales representatives, there is the question of
when the sale is "complete"; is it when there is a handshake, when a
purchase order is signed, when the product is delivered, or when the
bill is paid?

Finally, many bonus plans are predicated on the idea that the
individual must be an employee as of a certain date (most commonly
December 31 of the bonus year) to be eligible for any bonus. This
obviously presents a problem for anyone being fired on a date inconsistent with the end of the bonus calculation period. In addition,
there is the question of how to define the cutoff date for bonus calculations. Here's an example of the problem.

Susan Waters participates in a bonus program that is tied to the
calendar year performance of the company and of herself. She is fired
on December 3 and gets four months of severance pay starting on that
date. Her employer says she is entitled to no bonus whatsoever because she did not "work" the full calendar year and was not an "employee" on December 31. Susan feels that she is due at least a portion
of her bonus, given that she actually worked for the company for
eleven of the twelve months, and in addition points out that she will
remain on the payroll until the end of March of the following year,
thus satisfying both the calendar year employment requirement and
the December 31 requirement. Which side is right?

The answer is that there is no answer. Logic suggests that Susan
has a good point: She worked for the company for most of the year,
so she ought to get some of her bonus. On the other hand, the com-

pany may have a set of rules that it has applied in the past, and that excludes situations like Susan's from bonus eligibility.

A reminder on one of the key points of this chapter: No company is obligated to pay you severance of any kind unless it has a written policy that guarantees it. This is a negotiation. So you must take a practical approach when it comes to items like bonuses.

The Right Associates survey mentioned in Figure 1 makes it clear that *continuation* in a bonus plan is very unlikely after a termination; only 14 percent of senior executives and much smaller percentages of lower-level employees continue participation after they have been terminated (that is, during the period when their severance is being paid).

As in the remainder of your negotiations, the right approach here is the "package" approach. If your salary continuation is not what you hoped for, especially if it is based on some weeks-per-years-of-service calculation, you may be able to make a strong case for a full or partial bonus payment. You also probably have a stronger case if the reasons for your termination are other than performance-related; it is tough to make the case that you "earned" your bonus when you are being terminated for failing at the job.

Pension Plans and Other Retirement Benefits

The rules governing pension plans would fill ten books the size of this one. A web of legislation governs the management of such plans, including the Employee Retirement Income Security Act of 1974 (ERISA) and the Older Workers Benefit Protection Act of 1991. The Pension Benefit Guaranty Corporation was set up by Uncle Sam to intercede in situations where a pension plan has effectively gone bankrupt. You are fully protected if you have been fired to prevent you from collecting your pension benefits. Precisely because of this detailed legislation, even small companies with pension plans (and there is no legal requirement whatsoever that any employer must offer a pension plan) have carefully drawn documents outlining the provisions of the plan. In the termination process, many employers will wave these documents to make the point that the plan is etched in stone and nonnegotiable.

Needless to say, this is ridiculous. The company is not going to rewrite the plan for you, and it is difficult to negotiate when you are part of a mass layoff. But in individual terminations, companies negotiate elements of the pension plan all the time.

One possibility is to negotiate for continued membership in the plan. If the plan is totally funded by the company, or if a contribution that you make is matched in some way by the company, you certainly want to stay in the plan for at least as long as your severance pay continues. This means that you should negotiate for continued membership in the plan, for continued contributions to the plan by the company on its regular schedule and in the customary amounts, and for matching any contributions you make using the regular formula.

If the plan has performed particularly well and it is a defined contribution plan (that is, the company contributes a specific amount or percentage each year and the ultimate payout is determined by the investment performance of the plan), you might want to negotiate for long-term membership in the plan even though you will no longer be an employee. Obviously the company will stop making contributions to your pension account once you go off the payroll, but ultimately you will get your payout. If the plan is a defined benefit plan (that is, the payout is tied to some formula based on earnings and years of service but does not vary with the investment performance of the plan manager), there is little argument for staying in the plan after you are off the payroll.

You want to make absolutely certain that the company does not simply send you the proceeds from your pension plan when you go off the payroll. Under new 1993 legislation, even though you are entitled to roll such payouts over into your IRA or the pension plan offered by your new employer, this rollover must not pass through your hands; it must be a direct rollover into the new plan. If this is not handled carefully, you may have an obligation to pay a 20 percent tax at the time of rollover. Although Congress was considering legislation in 1993 to repeal this provision, you must make certain that you understand the law at the time of your termination.

Unless you are a long-term employee, there are issues of vesting to be considered. Most plans require a certain term of membership (for example, ten years) for you to be fully entitled to benefits; this is called the vesting period. You may not have been an employee long enough to be vested at all, or you may be only partially vested. If your departure leaves you less than fully vested, it may be possible to negotiate for additional vesting; this is called vesting acceleration.

For example, you may have five years of vesting in a plan that requires ten years of employment for full vesting, and you may be able to negotiate for one or two years of acceleration. Alternatively, if the plan forbids this or if your employer is adamant about not bending the plan (which is usually the case when a lot of people are being terminated at once), you can use this loss of pension benefits as an argument for greater salary continuation or for a fuller payout of your bonus plan. Alternatively, you can certainly argue at least for the vesting to continue for the duration of your severance payments.

One area in which companies tend to be very cautious is in terminating employees who are very close to being vested in their pension rights but who will have no such rights at all if their employment is terminated. Under the rules of ERISA, terminating an employee to deprive that employee of his pension rights can result in drastic punishment for the company. It is very difficult to prove that someone has been terminated specifically for that reason, and only a very unsophisticated employer would actually terminate someone with no other reason in mind, but companies know that a judge or jury will interpret any such action very negatively and will tend to be accommodating in negotiating some pension vesting as a result.

Finally, you can often negotiate for retirement planning counseling as part of your severance package. According to the Right Associates survey, 19 percent of companies provided such counseling to terminated key executives, and at least 10 percent provided it to all levels of employee. Bigger companies tend to be more generous with this particular benefit.

It bears repeating that pension rules and the laws covering them are very complex. You should seek an expert if you have any doubts about your rights.

Health Insurance and Other Medical Benefits

For some people, this is the most important negotiating issue. Health insurance is expensive, difficult to get, and subject to the exclusion of coverage for existing medical conditions. Health care costs are rising more rapidly than any other, and the health care system is widely acknowledged to be in crisis. It is no surprise that the subject is a critical one to someone being terminated.

Until 1986, the continuation of health insurance was a serious issue. Fortunately, the federal government took some action. You should immediately familiarize yourself with the Consolidated Omnibus Budget Reconciliation Act of 1986 (COBRA). Under COBRA, you are given the option of purchasing continued health insurance coverage for eighteen months after you are terminated. The cost is roughly comparable to what was being paid previously by you and your employer in combination (specifically, you pay 102 percent of the actual cost); for some people, this means that the health insurance they were previously getting for free could cost several hundred dollars per month. This is expensive, especially for anyone who has lost his or her job, but it is better than going without insurance coverage.

COBRA has limitations. It typically is not offered to employees of companies with twenty or fewer employees. You must exercise your option to use COBRA within sixty days of termination. Employees of federal agencies have very limited access to COBRA benefits. And employees who are terminated for gross misconduct are ineligible under some circumstances.

Appendix I outlines the laws of each state. About twenty states have their own laws pertaining to health insurance coverage in terminations, and in some cases they are more liberal than COBRA. Check the listing for your state.

In spite of legal entitlements, however, there still are health insurance-related negotiation issues during a termination. The most obvious one is to negotiate for your employer to continue paying the cost of your health insurance, both so that you do not have to start spending extra money at the worst possible time and so that you do not start exhausting your COBRA benefits.

Smart companies are sensitive to this issue; unlike your other household expenses, which typically will stay the same or even decline when you are out of work, COBRA payments represent a major increase in your cash outflow. Therefore, it is often possible to negotiate for continued health insurance coverage during the period of your severance pay, and occasionally even for some period after your severance payments have been discontinued. The company also might agree to split these costs with you even if it will not pay them outright; in cases where you have already been paying for part of the cost of your health insurance, the company may continue to pay for the portion it was buying.

Higher-level employees often have other health-related benefits. The most common of these are annual physicals and reimbursement plans that bridge the difference between reimbursements by the health insurance plan and actual out-of-pocket costs (for example, the 20 percent or $1,000 deductible in many plans). Companies that provide some company-paid continuation of health insurance as part of a severance package are often willing to include the extra reimbursement plan too, and you can often negotiate for a physical examination as well.

As stated earlier, health-oriented benefits are ones about which companies are sensitive at the time of termination, both because they worry about the effect of the termination on your health and because they are especially vulnerable to bad publicity and internal employee relations problems if a fired employee becomes ill and ends up in difficult financial or personal circumstances as a result. This is an area where you have a great deal of leverage.

Stock Option Plans

The issues related to stock option plans are very similar to those relating to pension plans because they have vesting provisions of a very similar nature. Anyone who receives stock options, which in some companies is all employees, receives the right to buy shares of the company at a price that is fixed on the date of the stock option grant. If the value of the shares rises over time, the employee can exercise the option and get totally risk-free profit (on which taxes are due). If the value of the stock drops, the employee simply does not exercise the option. These options vest over time; in a typical plan, they might vest at 20 percent per year for five years. What this means is that if an employee is fired twenty-five months after receiving a stock option grant, she would be entitled to exercise just 40 percent of those options.

There are several stock option issues in the event of a termination. One is whether the vesting can be accelerated in any way, that is, whether the employee can be given additional vesting as a severance payment. This would be reasonably common in cases where the company is trying to conserve cash and is thus less than generous with salary continuation, but wishes to offset this with some other type of severance payment. It would also be common in cases where the employee is very close to a vesting trigger point, for example, has options that are eleven months old and that would vest for the first time in another month. In a case like this, the company might well fear a legal claim that the employee was terminated specifically to prevent vesting; this is difficult to prove, but companies know that they look bad when they fire someone under these circumstances and therefore will be especially cautious.

The other major negotiation point, as with retirement plans, is to get continuation of vesting during the period when severance payments are being made. This can be very consequential, especially in cases where severance pay lasts six months or even a year. It can be especially consequential where there is "cliff vesting," that is, where no stock vests for a lengthy period of time and then a great deal vests all at once ("falls off a cliff"). You obviously prefer to reach the cliff before your vesting cuts off.

Companies also have been known to continue vesting stock options even after severance pay stops, or to allow someone to keep his options (that is, not be forced to exercise them) over an extended period even when vesting does not continue.

A key issue in how hard you want to negotiate with regard to options is your perception of how the company is doing and is likely to perform in the near term. If your best guess is that things will not go well and the stock price is likely to suffer, negotiating for other elements of the severance package would be more important. If the company is doing well, or if you have a great deal of unvested profit in your stock options, then tough negotiating on this subject becomes more appropriate.

Finally, if you are losing your job because of a merger or acquisition, be sure to read the option plan document, which may provide for specific treatment of options in these circumstances. Also, if you learn that executives at higher levels are getting preferential treatment with regard to option vesting, you may be able to argue more convincingly for the same treatment.

Other Insurances

Companies these days offer a variety of types of insurance other than health insurance; the two most common are life insurance and long-term disability insurance. My philosophy on all insurance plans is essentially the same: Get them continued for as long as possible. Companies typically will continue all insurance plans for as long as severance payments are being made, for reasons not unlike those that apply to health insurance: If you become ill, disabled, or deceased while on the company payroll, the company is going to look terrible if it has discontinued the relevant insurance plan. As with health insurance, you should try to get these insurances extended beyond the severance pay period if at all possible, at least until you find new employment.

Accrued Vacation and Sick Days

Most companies have quite specific policies regarding this subject, but occasionally there is room for maneuvering. This is especially true if you have been one of those people who never stays home sick and never uses up all the vacation time coming to you.

Company formulas are usually quite straightforward: You accrue so many days of vacation per year (or per month or per quarter), you can accumulate a certain number, and you get paid for untaken days up to a certain maximum when you leave the company. There is no law requiring that employers pay you for unused vacation time or sick days unless the company has a policy to that effect.

If your company has no policy, any kind of negotiation is fair game. If there is a policy, you must be more creative. Maybe the company will agree to treat your vacation days as an extension of your employment rather than pay for them in a lump sum, thus extending the life of your insurance benefits and stock vesting. If they want to pay you a lump sum, maybe they will defer the payment to next year or pull it into this year, whichever helps your tax situation the most.

In some cases the policy itself can be bent. I have seen situations where an employee was paid for sixty days of untaken vacation rather than for just the maximum thirty days allowable under the policy; the justification was that the company had decided to farm out a certain task that historically had been done internally, and that the several employees displaced were being asked to leave under special circumstances. I have seen a number of cases where sick days were treated as if they had accrued because the employee was having some minor medical problems at the moment and might under ordinary circumstances have taken some sick days anyway. And there certainly have been circumstances where the company paid people for unaccrued vacation or sick days simply because the boss felt guilty over firing someone and insisted on a variance from the human resources department.

Treatment of Loans

It is not uncommon these days, especially among the higher ranks of management, for employees to have company loans. Typically, these are of two types: loans associated with relocation, most often to help the employee buy a house in a higher-cost housing area, and loans associated with the exercise of stock options.

These loans typically have quite specific provisions that deal with termination of employment; a common provision would be that the loan becomes due and payable upon termination of employment, and in all circumstances must be repaid by ninety days thereafter.

Companies tend to be very generous in bending these provisions. In many cases the only way you can repay the loan is to sell your house, which typically occurs only after you have accepted new employment (either because you relocate or because your new employer agrees to replace the loan you must repay with one of its own). I have seen very few cases where the old employers enforced these loan agreements to the letter, although they would be totally within their rights to do so. It should not be difficult to get compromise on this one.

It is also possible in some cases to negotiate for some loan forgiveness, that is, for elimination of all or part of the loan. Keep in mind, however, that this is a double-edged sword, as any loan that is forgiven immediately becomes taxable income to you in the year of forgiveness, at a time when there is no cash flowing into your hands with which to pay the taxes. (What typically occurs in this case is that you take out a bank loan for the amount of the taxes and pay it back much as you would have paid off the prior loan.)

Perquisites

Most employees have perquisites of some kind, and senior-level employees often have many. These can be as mundane as the use of a company-subsidized cafeteria or as grand as country club memberships. Arrayed along this continuum are such things as tax planning reimbursement, discounts on company products or services, use of a company car, company-paid attendance at trade shows, company-subsidized day care, matching of charitable or educational gifts, tuition reimbursement plans, legal services, and use of a company exercise room. Although all these are very attractive, most are by their nature either more frivolous or at least less essential than the types of programs and benefits discussed earlier. You should use your judgment as to whether or not to press for keeping any of these, and should be prepared to make a logical case as to why they are important.

Here are some examples of logical arguments that have worked in the past:

- A single parent (or working mother) will find it difficult to search for a job without the availability of day care.
- An executive whose country club membership is paid for through the end of the year anyway would benefit by being able

to use the country club as a way of meeting prospective employers.

- An employee of an office products company wants to be able to buy stationery and supplies cheaply for résumé and letter preparation.
- An employee wants to attend a trade show to network with other industry executives during her job search.
- A manager who is in the middle of a company-subsidized MBA program wants to complete the semester without having to absorb the tuition cost.

Our focus thus far has been on not losing anything, that is, on negotiating to keep the major elements of your compensation and benefits package for as long after termination as possible. Chapter 5 focuses on those items the need for which is triggered by the termination itself and which have not previously been part of your compensation and benefits package.

Chapter 5

Adding to Your Existing Package

In Chapter 4, I discussed existing compensation and benefit plans already in your possession that you want to have continued to whatever extent possible. But there is another category of "benefit" that is created by the fact of your being fired. These benefits are contained in few employment contracts, and most of them are items you would probably never think about until you found yourself in the middle of a termination. Let's take each in turn.

Relocation Back to Your Place of Origin or to a New Site

Maybe you took your current job at a satellite office of your company, having transferred from the headquarters in Chicago to a branch in Duluth. Or maybe, when you first joined your current company, it moved you from your longtime home in Seattle to its offices in Portland, Oregon. Or maybe the company is located in a very small town where, as a practical matter, there are no job opportunities for someone with your skills.

In all these cases, it is worth trying to negotiate for a relocation allowance. Of course, this is a topic you should have raised at the time you took your current job. It is pretty much a given, for example, that employers who move employees overseas (whether they are new hires or internal transfers) will move them back to the United States if the job does not work out. But when the move has been within the United States, it is usually up to you to bring up the subject at the time of the move.

If you do not have such an agreement in advance, you must decide how important this benefit would be to you and therefore how hard you want to push for it. If you moved from New York to Chicago, it is going to be difficult to make the case that you lack career opportunities in Chicago, so you are probably better off negotiating for something else. If you moved from New York to Bangor, Maine, however, now at least you have a leg to stand on. And if the move from New York to Bangor was an internal transfer, your leverage is even greater.

Keep in mind that this is one of those negotiating items that may well have to be traded off against another. This still may work to your benefit. Certain relocation expense reimbursements are tax-free, whereas all direct severance pay is taxable. It is also true that relocation costs to take a new job are for the most part deductible, so you must do the arithmetic to calculate how you come out best. There are a number of arguments you can use that could help support your case:

- Your spouse moved with you and gave up his or her lucrative job in the originating city.
- You moved to the current location in order to get special training, which everyone understood was necessary to advance into positions available back at headquarters.
- You had a promise, however vague, that this was to be a short-term assignment and that soon you would be on to other things at other locations.
- You had to disrupt the educations and lives of your high-school-age children to go through this move in the first place.
- You would never have agreed to move if anyone had suggested that there was the slightest possibility your job was in jeopardy.

Office Services

At one level, this perk is a relatively harmless item. It involves a request for such job search assistance as typing services from your former secretary or a typing pool, phone answering services, the printing of your résumés, an office from which to make your calls and in which you can receive them, use of a telephone credit card, continued use of the voice mail system, and even reimbursement for travel expenses associated with your job search.

Many companies, especially large ones, have established an elaborate system to provide these services, including a special part of the building set aside for such job seekers to use. You can be sure that any such location will be very isolated from existing employees. Usually these locations have very unflattering nicknames, none of which are endorsed by the company; I have seen ones named "The Graveyard" and "The Visiting Team Bullpen" and have heard of lots of others.

Other companies provide these services indirectly through outplacement firms; this is discussed in the next section. Still other companies think the whole idea is terrible and do nothing. On balance, companies are becoming less enthusiastic about providing office space on company premises for terminated employees.

Much depends on your own frame of mind. You need to ask yourself how it will feel to come to your old place of work every day, often bumping into people who know your situation, and knowing yourself that the company really doesn't want you there anymore. You also need to decide how you feel about having the company in the middle of your job search. No matter how loyal to you they may be, the people typing your letters and answering your phone still work for the company, and their first allegiance is to their employer. In short, continuing to go to work every day can be awkward at best and downright depressing in many cases.

My own philosophy is that you are best served by negotiating for the out-of-pocket expenses (for printing résumés, telephone credit cards, and so on) but arranging for your own outside services. (The one exception would be if you had a personal secretary and can get permission for her to continue answering your phone for you. There is value to maintaining the pretense that you still work at the company, which in a legal sense you do while you are still on the payroll, so long as you do not have to walk into the office every day and confront those who still work there.)

I have heard a counterargument to this position, namely, that people who have been fired *are* better served if they can arrange to keep going to the office. The argument is that it is less of a disruption to their normal life pattern, that their co-workers for the most part will be sympathetic, and that the family will not be confronted all day long with tangible evidence of an unemployed parent or spouse. I understand this argument, and it probably is the right choice for some people, but my observation is that most people are more miserable doing it this way than they are confronting the hard realities of the situation and taking care of themselves. I might add that not one potential employer in a hundred is going to be fooled by this charade; it becomes obvious pretty quickly during the job-hunting process that you are in the process of leaving your past employer. Any company you can fool on this subject probably doesn't have people who are smart enough in it to make it a good prospective employer.

Outplacement and Retraining

An increasingly popular benefit offered to fired employees is the service of an outplacement firm. The Right Associates survey cited earlier reports that 69 percent of key executives, 55 percent of managers, 36 percent of supervisors, and 30 percent of administrative and technical personnel are offered these services as part of a severance package.

Years ago this was a relatively useless benefit, as the outplacement companies were populated mostly by sympathetic ears who would help you write and mail your résumé but do little else for you. In recent years, however, the outplacement industry has become much more professional, and many large and medium-size companies have ongoing relationships with one or more good outplacement firms. The best of them involve themselves with top management and with the human resources department even before a termination or layoff takes place, can counsel management on how to handle terminations, and are ready to step in without a break in the action.

As a result, there is little reason for not seeking this service from your employer, and it is such a good guilt-reducer for the company that has fired you that it will usually give it to you without argument. Often you don't even have to ask.

Outplacement firms can be very helpful to you in several ways. Many of us can use that sympathetic ear after going through a firing, and the sympathetic ear you find at home has a different feel to it than the one you get from a business professional. Outplacement firms know that people who have worked all their lives need to keep working, and they have real skill at getting you involved in the job search process immediately rather than sitting around brooding about the vicissitudes of life.

In addition, outplacement firms are much more knowledgeable than you are about the career-changing process, which is much more complicated than the job-changing process. Many people at inflection points in their careers want to consider something totally different but do not know how to do so; the outplacement firm can be extremely helpful in this respect. The statistics I have seen suggest that between 10 percent and 20 percent of the people who go through the outplacement process start their own businesses and about 75 percent go to work in a generally similar position in a new company. More than half of those who join a new company join a company smaller than the one at which they were employed previously.

Besides the aforementioned guilt avoidance, employers have a variety of reasons to opt for financing your outplacement. There is a lot of evidence that employees who are provided this benefit are less likely to sue their past employer, both because they are likely to find new employment faster and because they know it is hard to claim that they have been treated badly when their ex-employer has tried so hard to be helpful. Also, the more quickly you find a new position, the more quickly your severance pay and extended benefits will stop, thus saving your ex-employer a great deal of money (not that outplacement is cheap; a typical fee is 12 percent to 20 percent of the employee's previous year's compensation). You are less likely to exhaust your severance pay and file for unemployment compensation, which filing increases your employer's unemployment insurance rates. Companies also know that the employees still working for them are less likely to experience a drop in morale after a layoff if they know that the fired employees are treated well.

Indeed, some companies believe so fervently in the advantages for them (not to mention the advantages for you) of outplacement that in effect they insist on your participation by tying the continuation of your severance pay to your willingness to be "outplaced."

In addition to advice, many outplacement firms offer you an office to use, telephone and secretarial services, and the use of reference books. The exact level of service provided depends entirely on how much money your ex-employer wants to spend, and ranges from one-time meetings to lengthy counseling sessions and executive-quality office support. But keep in mind that outplacement firms will not find you a job nor will they guarantee that you will find one on your own; they exist to facilitate the learning process required so that you can find a job yourself.

In summary, outplacement is a relatively common termination-related benefit, and you should press hard for it if it is not volunteered. One word of warning: Keep in mind that your ex-employer is paying the outplacement firm's fee. If you divulge something that would be of interest to your former employer, such as the fact that you plan to file a lawsuit, there is every likelihood that this information will end up back in your ex-employer's hands. An ethical outplacement counselor should not do this, but it happens all the time. Therefore, tread cautiously in divulging anything that might be controversial.

A somewhat related benefit is some retraining allowance. This could be as simple as tuition for a refresher course in your field of employment or as complex as full payment for a complete career re- training program. Your leverage is highest if you have already em- barked on such a program, but there are instances (such as with laid- off workers in the aerospace industry) in which employers have fi- nanced broad-based training programs to help former employees re- direct their careers.

Negotiated Agreement on the Reference Story

Quality references get you jobs; poor ones make it almost impossible. You must have a conversation with your boss about what he or she will say. This conversation should be with your boss even though your exit negotiations may be with someone else, most likely some- one from human resources. Very few human resources departments provide substantive references, unless you are a senior executive and the vice president of human resources has had a personal working relationship with you. Most references come from the person to whom you reported directly.

The critical point to remember is that you are being asked to leave the company. This may be totally your fault or may have nothing whatsoever to do with you personally; people who lose their jobs in a layoff owing to lack of seniority certainly cannot be faulted. Never- theless, you need a mechanism for defusing the doubts that inevita- bly arise in the mind of a prospective new employer when he sees that you are out of work. One of these mechanisms is your reference checks.

For middle- and lower-level jobs, it never hurts to ask for a letter of reference. These letters usually don't count for much because no one ever writes anything critical in them, but in a situation where your departure is easily explainable and not due to your performance, the letter will suffice for some prospective employers and thus shorten the job search process. The lower the level of the job, the more likely it is that such letters will be useful.

If you have been in a more senior position, reference letters are essentially useless, although you may be offered the chance to write your own and there is no reason to avoid this task. You might as well be extremely complimentary while you're at it! If you are a senior executive, however, remember that any company that uses reference letters to evaluate you (and skips the reference-calling process) is a company that doesn't know how to hire people, and is to be avoided. Just think what the other people in the company must be like if that kind of amateurish hiring process has been used.

Some companies and bosses will tell terminated employees that the reference-checking question is a moot one because of a company policy that forbids reference checks. Such companies say that they will only confirm someone's dates of employment. There are indeed companies that have such policies, usually born of fear of litigation from ex-employees who could claim that they were prevented from getting employment by bad references (we talk more about this "defamation" issue in Chapter 9). One survey showed that 41 percent of human resources professionals said that their companies had formal policies not to provide references.

Do not believe this argument for one second! I have checked thousands of references in my life and can count on one hand the number of executives who refused to give me reference checks on former employees. Even those few were people who had terrible things to say and didn't feel like saying them. In no case have I ever reached a potential reference on the phone who refused to give me at least some information. Yet hundreds of these people worked for companies that theoretically do not provide references.

Occasionally it takes some creative questioning, but something germane always comes out. There simply is an unwritten code in the business world that reference information is shared, and you must assume that your prospective employer will check these references.

So how can you affect this process? The answer is that you may not be able to affect it very much, but every little bit helps. I would suggest that while you are conducting your negotiation interview with your boss, or whenever you and your boss have your last conversation, you should bring up the subject of reference checks. You can say something like this: "I'm sure that all my potential employers are going to ask me for your name for the purpose of checking references. I need to understand what you are going to say to them so that I won't get caught by surprise."

The rest of this conversation depends greatly on the circumstances of your firing and what your boss says next. If you are being laid off for seniority reasons, your boss will probably say that he will be very complimentary and will explain to everyone that he would like to have kept you in the company, that your work was as good or better than that of others with more seniority who retained their jobs, and so on. This type of reference obviously poses no problem.

If you are being fired for poor performance or for personal chemistry conflicts, however, the way in which the story gets told is very important. Keep in mind that no one is ever going to tell you that you didn't get a job because your ex-boss gave you a bad reference; that would violate rule 1 of the reference-checking game, which requires that information given in references be kept confidential. So it is most important that you have a very specific conversation with your boss in these circumstances.

Let's say that you are being fired because your work output was not what your boss wanted it to be. Rather than your boss saying it just that way, you could negotiate with her to say something like the following: "Bob was in one of those roles with an enormous require-ment for output. He works very hard, and in the past did a very good job. In this case I feel we put him in a job that was wrong for him, keeping track of a large amount of administrative detail. Bob is very good with the big picture and with projects of any type. He is proba-bly less well suited to tasks where there are hundreds of daily details to be checked."

Is this a glowing reference? No. Will it support your candidacy for every kind of job? Also no. But it *will* support your candidacy for certain kinds of jobs, and by being balanced it has the ring of truth, which hopefully it is. Again, keep in mind that a skilled reference checker is not going to be fooled. People who check a lot of references know how to ask leading questions, how to listen for intonations and words with special meanings, how to "triangulate" (that is, ask the same questions of multiple people and listen for differences in the answers, and then call certain references back with those differences and ask for an interpretation), how to dig deeper, how to gather rel-ative information in addition to absolute information so that positive adjectives will be put in context. *The odds that you can keep concealed the fact that you were fired are infinitesimal.*

So what you must do is get your ex-boss to agree to put the most positive spin on things without lying. Often you can get your boss to agree not to volunteer certain negatives unless asked. She may be willing to emphasize certain real points of strength or to downplay points of weakness. She may be willing to say that your departure was by "mutual agreement" and to elaborate on why you both felt it was time for you to move on. (I am of two minds about the phrase *mutual agreement;* 99 percent of the time it means "fired" and everyone knows it, but some people giving references are very good at making the case that a decision to separate was reached together.)

All this assumes that your firing was for generally acceptable rea-sons. If you were fired for what is known as "cause," typically for some major infraction like stealing from the company or continually coming to work drunk, don't spend a lot of time on this part of the conversation with your boss. Most companies in these circumstances simply won't give reference checks, and those doing the reference checking know that something pretty terrible must have happened if everyone holds to the "no reference check" policy.

One final point here. Merely by bringing up the subject, you put your ex-boss on notice that you know about reference checks, that you will be watching the process, and that you are sensitive to the issues (legal issues, that is, though you never want to mention lawsuits or the law) inherent in the reference-checking process. This is often enough to exert a moderating influence on any negatives.

Unemployment Eligibility

Every state has an unemployment insurance program to which employers contribute (I never understood the word *contribute,* because it is far from voluntary; essentially, it is a payroll tax). In most cases, as an unemployed person you are entitled to up to twenty-six weeks of compensatory pay, and there are circumstances when this time period is extended by the federal government.

Your employer, however, does not especially want you to put in an unemployment compensation claim. The reason for this is simple: Each employer contributes to the unemployment insurance system according to a formula that is based in part on the number of claims made by its ex-employees. The more who file, the more your ex-employer pays. For this reason, your employer may try to induce you to agree not to apply for unemployment. The two most common inducements are to give you some extra severance pay and to agree to "let you resign" and to tell the world (here we are back to reference checking again) that you quit voluntarily.

The reason for this latter inducement is that people who quit voluntarily without a good reason are not eligible for unemployment benefits. In fact, in most states you can lose your eligibility for several reasons:

- You quit your job without a good reason.
- You are fired for misconduct (sometimes it must be "repeated willful misconduct").
- You are fired for "just cause" (stealing, hitting a supervisor, drunkenness on the job, etc.).

- You are fired for striking illegally.
- You refused to accept a similar job without good reason.
- You retire voluntarily.
- You are in jail.

On the other hand, in some states there are circumstances under which you can quit and still be eligible for unemployment, for instance, if you have been harassed sexually or racially, if your job is endangering you, if your duties or pay have been changed for the worse in some meaningful way, or if in some other sense you have been "constructively discharged" (see Chapter 2).

If none of these apply to you, however, you must decide how to approach the unemployment insurance issue. Obviously you prefer to keep your eligibility. Your severance pay has a limited life (you cannot collect unemployment benefits while receiving severance pay unless the severance pay was part of a deferred pay plan in which you were participating), and that limited life may run out before you have a new position. On the other hand, some companies will really try hard to induce you not to file for benefits.

In general, I do not feel that you should sign away your unemployment insurance rights. The future is simply too hard to predict. However, it is worth considering trading away these benefits if all of the following circumstances exist:

- Your job prospects are good.
- Your severance program is generous, and is supplemented by severance pay for a longer period than the original offer as an inducement for you not to file for unemployment.
- Your employer agrees that your records will show that you quit voluntarily, and your boss agrees to support this story in references.

You should note that your employer may have a separate agenda here as well. If the records show that you quit, and if you sign a document (which the company certainly will want you to do) saying that you quit, it will be almost impossible for you to win a wrongful discharge lawsuit if you decide to file one. After all, it is tough to claim that you were wrongfully discharged if you were not discharged. This will be discussed in more detail in later chapters, and it may be irrelevant to you if you have no desire to sue anyone, but you should keep in mind that you will complicate your case by such an action.

If your employer does not bring up the unemployment insurance subject at all, you should negotiate for an agreement that your unemployment claim will not be contested if you need to make one.

Service Letters

There is no U.S. law that requires your employer to explain to you why you were fired. Most employers will make some passing effort to do so, if only because you will probably be furious if you are fired without explanation and thus more likely to file a lawsuit.

Several states require an employer to provide what is known as a service letter, describing your work history and (sometimes) the reason for your departure. These include Kansas, Maine, Minnesota, Missouri, Montana, Nevada, Texas, and Washington. If you live in such a state, you should request this letter upon termination if it is not volunteered. Keep in mind that this request must be made quickly, in some cases as soon as five days after termination, and typically must be made in writing.

If you live in a state without such a law, I think it is a good idea to request a written explanation for your firing anyway. Some companies will simply refuse to provide one, and there is little you can do other than to ask until you are tired of asking.

On the other hand, having such a letter will be helpful with some prospective employers, and it is one more document for your files in case there is future litigation. Most companies are eager to get fired employees out the door, and may agree quickly to such a letter and probably even write it more positively than you might expect just to avoid aggravation.

If your company refuses, you should write a brief letter after your departure. It should be polite and free of aggressive language. In it, you should say that you are writing to clarify the reasons for your termination; then you should state that you understand you were terminated for some set of reasons (that is, list the reasons), and that you wish to be advised in writing within two weeks if the company disagrees with the reasons you have listed. Although it really does not prove much if the company does not reply, you can argue later that it must have agreed if it decided not to take issue with your letter. If it does reply, then you have the information you wanted in the first place.

Your letter should be sent by certified mail with return receipt requested so you can prove that it was received by the company. The use of certified mail also sends a signal to the company about how important the subject is to you.

Personnel File

Ideally, you obtained your personnel file a long time ago as part of your self-protection campaign if you saw a termination coming. However, not all of us can see the future so clearly, and in some cases there simply are no signals. Or you may have bought this book after the termination took place.

In any event, if you don't have a copy of your personnel file, request it as part of the termination negotiations. You might learn something if the company refuses to hand it over, though the laws of your state must be taken into account (see Appendix I). Refusal to show you your file could mean that your employer knows it has weak documentation for its case to fire you. But it could also mean that the company just doesn't like to hand out files, so be cautious about jumping to conclusions if you live in one of those states where employee access to files is not guaranteed.

Be prepared for the fact that there are rules regarding personnel files. For example, even in those states that give you access to the files, you must often make the request in writing; you should bring a written request to your termination interview. You should also request a copy of the file, though you may not get it.

Especially in those states where there is no law requiring access to your file, this is your moment of greatest leverage. Your boss is already embarrassed by the termination process and wants to get you off his hands as soon as possible. He is more apt to be agreeable to requests like this now than he will be at any future moment. In wrongful discharge litigation (see Chapter 9), a crucial issue can be the "paper trail" that the company has assembled. In plain English, has it substantiated the reasons for your firing? Were you given poor performance evaluations and other warnings? Would a reasonable person have understood that his job was in jeopardy?

If not, you have a much stronger case if it ever comes to litigation. And all of this should be in your personnel file.

Chapter 6

What the Company Wants From You

Like all negotiations, termination negotiations have two players and two points of view. Chapters 4 and 5 focused on the things you want from the company. But there are things the company wants from you. Some of these you may be happy to give, especially as a quid pro quo for something else. Others are to be avoided like the plague.

As previously discussed in Chapter 5, it is in your employer's best interest to have you agree not to file for unemployment compensation. If you are starting your reading at this point in the book, go back and read that section. In this chapter, I want to take up some other concessions your employer may hope to get from you.

Non-Compete Agreements

A non-compete agreement or non-compete clause stipulates that you may not go to work for a competitor or start a competitive business for some specified period of time. There may also be a geographic boundary associated with such agreements, permitting you to engage in competitive activity just so long as it is outside the geographic area served by your ex-employer. What an employer is attempting to do is to prevent its employees from going elsewhere and competing with them.

No federal law permits or prohibits or even discusses such agreements. Several states prohibit or limit them in some way (see Appendix I), but for the most part you are on your own in negotiating with your employer on this topic.

Many companies require the signing of non-compete agreements at the time new employees are hired. Essentially, you have no choice about this if you want the job. You should keep in mind, however, that a very broad and long-lasting non-compete clause will probably not be enforceable in the courts, although there is nothing to prevent your employer from suing you to try and enforce it.

If you signed a non-compete agreement upon hiring, now is the time to try and have it voided. You can accurately point out to your employer that you will be most attractive as an employee to companies in businesses in which you have experience, and to foreclose this possibility will undoubtedly prolong your unemployment and need for severance pay. In some cases, especially if your company is firing you for what it feels are poor performance reasons, it may be motivated to void the prior agreement on the basis that you pose no threat to them. You may find this insulting, but grin and bear it; you will have achieved your objective of eliminating an obstacle to new employment.

If you did not sign such an agreement upon starting work, your employer may try to get you to sign one now. There is no way that you can be forced to do so, though there may be inducements that make you willing to consider it seriously. Employers have been known to make the availability of severance pay contingent on the signing of such an agreement.

Every case is different, so there are no simple rules of thumb. Obviously it is best for you not to be constrained in any way from seeking employment. If the non-compete clause seems like a major issue to your ex-employer, and if the loss to you (of severance pay or whatever) in not signing is considerable, you should negotiate for the most limited terms possible.

Other than in very special circumstances (such as when an owner sells a company and is constrained from competing with the acquirer), it would be very unusual to exceed one year as the non-compete period, and the clock should start ticking immediately (that is, when you leave the premises of your ex-employer, not when your severance pay runs out). Likewise, the geography should be as limited as possible. If you work for a company that conducts all its business in the northeastern United States, it would be foolish for them to insist on a non-compete agreement that applies to the whole country, and no court would endorse such a program.

In fact, courts generally frown on the idea of non-compete agreements and are becoming increasingly less sympathetic to them. In California, a state generally sympathetic to employees, these agreements are virtually unenforceable unless you have sold a company to someone or unless all your stock in your employer has been bought

back. Even in states that allow them, there usually must be some com-
pelling reason, like the protection of trade secrets.

Non-compete agreements somehow fly in the face of our beliefs
in freedom of movement and the free enterprise system. Most courts
will interpret them very narrowly and with a focus on the proprietary
information of your employer (or, even more likely, on a narrower
class of information known as trade secrets), and generally will permit you to work where you please as long as safeguards as to this
confidential information are in place. Most courts would also insist
that you receive something of real value (like lengthy extended severance pay) in return for limiting your employment opportunities.

If you are subject to a non-compete agreement, you must consider carefully how to act. But you should not prevent yourself from
making a thorough job search. The fact that you worked for a steel
company and have agreed not to work for another steel company
means that you should be able to work for an aluminum company,
even if that company makes products that compete with those of your
ex-employer. The fact that you have agreed not to sell property and
casualty insurance in Memphis does not prevent you from selling it
in Nashville, or from selling some other kinds of insurance in Memphis. You might even be able to sell property and casualty insurance
in Memphis if your ex-employer sold only to certain kinds of customers and you go to work for a company with a different target customer. The key here is to get your non-compete clause defined as
narrowly as possible.

Non-Recruit Agreements

When employees depart, the biggest fear of some employers is that
the ex-employee will land a new job and immediately start recruiting
away their best people. This is especially a concern when someone
has been fired and may feel vindictive.

As part of a non-compete agreement, your company therefore
may try to get you to sign a document stating that you will not recruit
away its people. If you have no intention of doing so anyway, this is
not a big issue. However, keep in mind that your attractiveness to a
potential new employer may in part rest on your ability to quickly
attract a team of people to work with you. This is especially true if
you are a sales executive.

As a result, you want to be cautious about signing non-recruit
agreements. They should certainly be of short duration, at the very

longest one year. You also need to clarify the treatment of one specific situation: the case where an employee of your ex-employer approaches you about a new position.

There is no legal or practical way that an employer can prevent an employee from quitting. If you are approached by one of your former colleagues who wants to leave his current employer to join you, it is unreasonable for you to be constrained from hiring that person. You should therefore negotiate an understanding in your non-recruit agreement that you will not actively approach your former co-workers for some specific period of time, but are free to hire anyone who approaches you first.

Now, your ex-employer is not stupid. The company knows that if it agrees to such a provision, you could approach one of its employees, concoct a story saying that the employee approached you first, and then proceed to hire that person with seeming impunity. However, most companies realize that indentured servitude went out of style a long time ago, and that they really can't do much to prevent the recruiting process anyway. After all, you could strike a deal with one of your former colleagues, he could go in and quit on some basis or other, and two weeks later you could hire him and claim that he was out of work and no longer an employee of your former employer.

Would this be a subterfuge? Of course. But since it is so easy to do, most companies will go along with a reasonably balanced non-recruit agreement if they insist on one at all.

One major word of caution here: If your ex-employer sues you for recruiting away its employees in violation of a non-recruit agreement, keep in mind that those employees are unlikely to perjure themselves if questioned by attorneys in a deposition. The fact that you induced them to quit with a promise of a job is unlikely to stay hidden if legal action is initiated.

Non-Disclosure Agreements

Companies possess all kinds of information that they look upon as confidential. This includes trade secrets, customer lists, proprietary formulas, even special interviewing techniques. Much of this information is less secret than the company believes, but the belief in its confidentiality is strongly held nonetheless.

Chances are that you were asked to sign a confidentiality agreement when you joined the company. This would have required you to agree never to divulge anything confidential that you learned while employed there, and probably stated that any inventions or discoveries in which you participated become the property of your employer.

If you did not sign any such agreement at the outset, you almost certainly will be asked to sign one as you leave. If the wording refers to "trade secrets," you are constrained by the laws of most states from divulging these to anyone whether you sign anything or not, so you aren't limiting yourself by signing. If the wording is broader and merely refers to "confidential information" or "proprietary information," most good employment attorneys will advise you not to sign, because the definition of these concepts may be extended too broadly by an ex-employer paranoid about its data or trying to make your life difficult. If confronted with this broader language, you must simply weigh the benefits of signing versus the constraints it may place on you. This is often a situation where some advice from a good attorney would be helpful.

There is a second kind of confidentiality agreement that many companies propose to departing employees. This is an agreement stating that you will not discuss with anyone the issues surrounding your departure or the terms of your severance payments (or even that you got any severance), and that you will not disparage the company or its employees in any way.

The motivations of your employer in asking you to sign such an agreement are several. The company doesn't want other employees to know how much severance pay you received, especially if it is an individually crafted severance package as opposed to one derived from a formal written severance plan. If you are a senior executive and likely to be interviewed by the press, it doesn't want you speaking critically of the company. It doesn't want you giving information to competitors about its hiring and firing practices. In the final analysis, odd as it seems, firings are as difficult and embarrassing for the company doing the firing as for the employee being fired, and the company wants the whole process to be as quiet as possible. Fortunately, this is what gives you part of your negotiating leverage.

Signing this kind of non-disclosure agreement should not be a very big deal to you unless you are determined to vent your spleen to the outside world, but it is a bigger deal to your employer. Chances are that you would not bad-mouth your former employer anyway; any book on interviewing techniques will tell you that this is a bad idea because it brands you in the eyes of prospective employers as a complainer and malcontent. As a result, since you should be relatively indifferent to signing such a clause, you can use this part of the negotiation to your advantage. This is the point at which you can get the company to agree to skew your references positively, or at which you can negotiate for a bit more severance pay or benefits.

Waiver of the Right to Sue

This is the most insidious of the items your ex-employer will want from you, and they will want it very badly. In fact, a lot of companies try to slip it into the conversation at the moment of your firing, when you may be upset and worried about the future.

This waiver, also known as a "covenant not to sue," simply states that you agree not to sue your ex-employer. It may be totally harmless if you have no intention of suing anyway. On the other hand, you have not yet fully thought out your treatment in the termination process, and to sign away this right makes little sense. In fact, the company cannot simply ask you to give up this right. It is quite clear in the law that *in exchange for such an agreement, the company must give you something that you would not otherwise get.*

To be more specific, it is not allowable for the company to induce you to sign such a document in exchange for accrued vacation pay, severance pay, or anything else if these things are due you under a formal company plan or if it has been the common practice to give such benefits and payments to other departing employees. If the company has announced a severance plan as part of a major layoff, this is something to which you are already entitled, and thus it cannot be used to satisfy the requirements for some kind of compensation in exchange for a release from your legal right to sue.

The courts are very stringent about this, because the concept of signing away your legal rights is carefully scrutinized in the law. To repeat, the principle is very simple: If you are to give up your rights to sue, your employer must induce you to do so with something extra that you would not otherwise have received. Litigation over discharge is common. In the Right Associates survey quoted in Chapter 4, 24 percent of responding companies said that they had been sued over severance programs. I suspect that the real percentage is even higher. It is a major concession on your part to relinquish this right.

Having said all this, I would nevertheless argue that it may still make sense to do so under some circumstances. You may simply not be the kind of person who sues. You may realize that you have no case anyway. A large inducement, such as a substantial increase in your severance pay, may be worth the trade-off. This is a very individual decision.

My advice, therefore, is simply not to sign this or any other document without consulting an attorney who specializes in employment law. The stakes are too large. If you have somehow been coerced into signing, keep in mind that there usually are revocability periods available. As you will see in future chapters, there are certain laws like the Older Workers Benefit Protection Act (for those over 40) that permit you to change your mind after signing documents like these. Your attorney can advise you.

Part Three
The Aftermath

Chapter 7

Protecting Yourself

Most employers are honorable in their dealings with fired employees. Yes, you see articles in the newspapers trumpeting all sorts of horror stories. And there certainly are dishonest people in every walk of life. But chances are that your employer will treat you fairly. Just don't be naïve.

You need to make sure that your former employer is living up to the promises made during the termination process. You also need to make sure that the company is not taking steps to make your life difficult. This will consume very little of your time; think of it as the equivalent of balancing your checkbook every month. Most of the time it will be wasted effort, but once in a while the process will uncover something really important. Here are eight steps you should take to protect yourself.

1. *Examine every severance payment carefully.* When you get your monthly or weekly severance paycheck, go over the numbers carefully. Did the withholding change in some way? Is the gross payroll amount correct? Are there any mistakes in your Social Security number, the spelling of your name, or any other information?

If your company is of any size, it uses an outside payroll service from its bank or from a company like ADP. Smaller companies often use payroll services also. Even if the company writes its own payroll checks, your termination triggered a whole set of record-keeping procedures that probably put you in a new category as far as the check writers are concerned. This creates the opportunity for clerical errors that you must nip in the bud. If you discover such errors after you are off the payroll, it is a major hassle to get them corrected.

2. *Examine every lump sum payment carefully.* There are a variety of payments you may receive that you have not gotten in the past. These include final bonuses, payouts from pension plans (lump sum or monthly), closeouts of company credit union accounts, final reim-

bursement of expense accounts, one-time special severance payments, and the like. Some of these payments, most notably pension payments, are the result of elaborate, actuarially based calculations.

Do not assume that these have been done correctly. Ask to be shown the actuarial tables on which your payment is based. Make sure that your final expense account was approved in full; companies often figure that they are on safe ground in applying more stringent expense accounting standards to fired employees. Examine the amount and tax withholding from your final bonus in the same way you did with your severance check. Look at the last credit union statement you got before you were fired and the first one sent you after you were fired; do they make sense when compared with one another?

3. *Submit all medical expenditures immediately.* If you have any unsubmitted expenses on the day you are fired, send them into the system right away. If you remain in the health insurance program for a while, submit each and every medical bill as it is incurred. Keep a careful accounting of every submitted expense and follow up quickly if it is not reimbursed.

There is little likelihood that anyone will try and cheat you with regard to medical insurance; in fact, medical claims processing is probably out of your employer's hands. The problem is like that with payroll checks. When you are fired, your employer typically notifies the insurance carrier (or the insurance department, if your company self-insures) that your health insurance will terminate as of a specific date. This again creates the opportunity for clerical error. Ultimately, you will get your money back even if you are locked out of the health insurance plan inadvertently, but the process of sorting out the mistake is very time-consuming.

4. *Save every piece of paper and make notes about every telephone conversation.* Be literal about this. If the company writes to you on any subject, save the envelope and letter. Save your payroll stubs, notes from the health insurance company, all credit union statements, copies of your application for unemployment benefits, employee handbooks, *anything.* I suggest getting an inexpensive accordion file and putting each document in its category.

If you have any conversation with anyone, no matter how trivial, write down what was said and put it in the file. You will find that you will have many such conversations about your benefits and compensation arrangements. Write down what your boss said to you when you were fired and what he says in subsequent conversations. Write down what the human resources department says. Write down what the insurance department says about making medical claims.

Especially important, write down what your former co-workers say about what is happening at the company, about other firings and layoffs, and about you.

The reason for all this record keeping is simple. First of all, you want to make sure that the company is living up to its obligations, and this is a simple way to keep track of what those obligations are. Second, in case you end up in litigation, you can be certain that the company has been keeping copious records of everything that has transpired. You have a much more powerful story if you can quote what a specific person said, with a date, time, and location as part of the record; this not only puts the company on the defensive but identifies you as a competent person who is unlikely to be making unsubstantiated claims.

5. *Talk to your former co-workers on a regular basis.* You want to know what is being said about you. You may have made an agreement during the termination process that your employer would keep the reason for your departure a secret. Regardless of any agreement made, you want to make certain that you are not being defamed.

You can conduct this process without interrogating people. You have friends from the company whom you see on a social basis; engage them in conversation about the old workplace, your old boss, and what impression is being given about you. If there is even the slightest clue that you are being defamed, dig deeper with your former co-workers. Write down everything, including the date and the name of the person who gave you the information. (However, do not write these things down as they are being told you; there is no more certain way to lose friends and to have them stop telling you what you need to know. Keep in mind that they want to hold on to their jobs, however sympathetic they may be that you lost yours.) Be very careful not to ask for or discuss anything that could be construed as a trade secret. If there are other people present when you have these conversations, write down their names as well; they can be corroborating witnesses later.

If you conclude that you are being defamed (go and read the section in Chapter 9 on defamation before jumping to this conclusion), consult an attorney.

6. *Get a copy of your personnel file.* You should have done this previously when you first read this book, and you certainly should have done it as part of the termination process if you were allowed to do

so. Do it again, preferably after about a month has passed. You want to see if anything has been put in the record regarding your termination that is incorrect or damaging and that might inadvertently be passed along to a future employer or be used against you (such as in a claim for unemployment insurance).

7. *Write in for employment history information.* This requires a bit of effort, but you can learn an unbelievable amount from the process. It is worth doing if you have the slightest concern about what is being said about you, or if you don't trust your past employer for any reason. Don't do it casually; do it only if you truly feel that an investigation is necessary. Consider having your attorney do it for you.

Just send in a letter to your old company saying that you are considering hiring yourself (obviously you use another name when signing the letter) and asking for an employment history and reference letter on yourself. A typical letter would look like the one shown in Figure 2.

Figure 2. Sample letter requesting reference and employment history.

Human Resources Department
XYZ Corporation
Middletown, USA

To Whom It May Concern:

We are considering employing Mr. William Thompson. As a prelude to this employment decision, we would appreciate receiving any relevant information from your records, including dates of employment, any breaks in service, reasons for his separation, and eligibility for rehire.

Thank you very much.

Herbert Wilson
Employment Supervisor

Any legitimate employer will respond to this kind of request. The human resources department may want to call first to verify who is writing to them, so you need a phone number and voice mail (available very inexpensively in most states from the phone company) to receive any such calls. Be sure not to use your own voice in the voice mail.

8. *If you have reason to believe that your ex-employer is violating your agreement regarding reference information about you, consider having someone check your references by phone.* This has some danger associated with it in that information gathered falsely may be construed as fraud, although it is unclear that anyone could prove damages. You should take this step cautiously, and not just because you are curious. But if you truly believe you are being defamed or misrepresented in violation of an agreement, it is worth considering. This is a case where you would be wise to consult an attorney first.

If you proceed, ideally there should be at least two calls. The most important one is to your former boss; the second one is to the human resources department. The latter one won't produce much in most cases, but the former one could be a gold mine.

What you are trying to determine is what your former employer is saying about you. The reference check should be conducted exactly as if the person calling is a prospective new employer or an employment firm working with you on a prospective new position.

Get someone who sounds credible and appropriate to do this, preferably someone who has checked references before. If you are truly convinced that your agreement concerning references has been breached, consider enlisting an attorney to help you with the call. Under absolutely no circumstances should you make the call yourself. Have your caller ask very specific questions, including but not limited to the following:

"Tell me about Bill's strengths and weaknesses."
"How would you characterize his interpersonal relations with you, his peers, and his subordinates?" (And if the conversation is with the human resources department, ask about Bill's relationship with the boss also.)
"On a scale of one to ten, how hard a worker would you say he is?"
"How effective was he at getting his work done on time within budget, and what was the quality of that work?"
"How did his subordinates feel about him? If they complained about him, what were the complaints?"

"Were there ever any questions about his integrity? His work habits? His work ethic? His personal habits as related to the workplace?"

"Why did he leave your employment?" (If you get a partial or inaccurate answer, follow up by saying that you know he was fired and asking why this happened.)

"What kind of job is Bill best suited for?"

"We are talking to Bill about a job as a [*name of appropriate job*]. Do you think this is the right kind of position for him?"

"Would you rehire Bill if you had the right opening?"

Keep in mind that prospective employers are going to make these kinds of phone calls. You just want to make sure that you know what is going to be said.

The point of this entire chapter is a simple one. Your prior employer has certain explicit and implicit obligations to you. The company must obey the law and it must deliver what it has promised. As stated earlier, most companies live up to their obligations to the best of their ability, so your objective here is merely to make certain that no administrative or inadvertent errors slip through the cracks. In cases where the company's intentions and ethics are less clear, your objective broadens to a more thorough job of due diligence, that is, making sure that you are not being cheated or mistreated.

Chapter 8

Firing and Your Emotions

Getting fired is one of the most difficult emotional experiences you can undergo, ranking below only such events as the death of an immediate family member, a major illness, or a divorce. To those of us whose identities are tied up in our work, it can be one of the most emotionally wrenching experiences of all.

Thomas Holmes and Richard Rahe developed an elaborate "Social Readjustment Rating Scale" that rated being fired very high on the stress scale, and that was at a time when the economy was strong and finding a new job was relatively easy. It can only be worse today.

Not surprisingly, the reactions to being fired are very much like those to any other serious emotional event. A sense of failure and inadequacy is inevitable. If you are like most people, you will have most or all of the following reactions to being fired:

Shock and Disbelief

"How can this be happening to me? People like me don't get fired. All those other people I know who have been fired . . . they deserved it. But me? This is ridiculous! They can't do this to me!"

These are normal reactions. Unless you are the exception, you weren't trying to get fired. You have a high opinion of yourself and you want to protect it. The view your company obviously has of you is inconsistent with the view you have of yourself, and you have no intention of changing your self-assessment.

By the same token, this can be a very immature reaction as well. The truth is that they *can* do it to you, like it or not. It may be unfair, it may be immoral, it may even be illegal, but in the final analysis your company can fire you if it feels like it. To have thought otherwise, or to think otherwise now, is to ignore the way the world works. And you ignore the world at your own peril.

Disbelief passes quickly, because it must. You need to find a new job. You need to get on with your life. You need to immerse yourself in the reality of extricating yourself from the old and getting on with the new, whatever that may be.

Anger

You feel furious that this has been done. Your source of income has been removed. You are embarrassed with your family and friends. Your whole emotional life has been thrown into upheaval. Your financial life is a potential disaster area. Of course you're angry!

Not to feel anger over an event that should make you feel angry is not to be alive. It is a perfectly normal reaction. And what you must do is talk about it with someone: a friend, a co-worker, a member of the clergy, an outplacement counselor, a therapist if you have one.

You will notice that I did not put your spouse at the top of this list. You should of course talk with your spouse first. But keep in mind that the loss of your job can be every bit as threatening and upsetting to your spouse as it is to you. Some marriages are damaged badly by job loss; in other cases, it's an opportunity to pull together as a team. This is very hard to predict, so you must tread cautiously and with sensitivity. Don't just assume that yours are the only frail emotions out there.

What you must avoid is keeping this anger inside. Not only will it eat away at you, it will also be transparent to potential future employers. No one who is seen as an angry person gets hired, especially if the anger is directed at a former employer. In fact, it is a rule of thumb in the hiring process that you don't hire someone who says bad things about his or her last company or boss.

Fear

Everyone has some fear of the unknown. Every terrible possibility occurs to you. Can you find another job? Will it pay as much as the last? Will you be able to make your mortgage or rent payments? Will you have to move? Will you lose your friends or your status in the community?

As you can see, many of these fears are related to cold hard cash.

Certainly your job provides you with ego satisfaction. But at a much more elemental level, it provides you with food and shelter. Anything that threatens these survival needs is inevitably going to make you afraid.

The reaction to fear in animals takes one of two forms: fight or flight. The zebra can try to kick the lion to death, or can try to outrun it. Whereas zebras tend to lose these particular confrontations, you are a lot more adaptable and resilient.

Fighting can take two forms. The useless form is to fight your employer. Nothing short of litigation over some wrongful discharge is going to get you your job back. Calling people names, complaining to a higher executive, or firebombing the company cafeteria also aren't going to get you anywhere.

The potentially productive form of fighting is to direct your energies to the job search process. Get yourself organized and moving. Write the résumé today. If you have outplacement benefits, schedule your first appointment right now. Get yourself started on a new path. At the same time, fight for severance and fair treatment in the ways outlined in this book.

The "flight" syndrome is a dangerous one. You must resist the tendency to take a month off, to delay sending out résumés, to hope that the one job prospect you have will be the right one and thus put off pursuing others. You must avoid fleeing from the task at hand: to find a new job.

This is easy enough to say. But depression is often a part of the emotional reaction to being fired; this is the subconscious way in which our brain allows flight. Many is the fired person who all of a sudden doesn't feel well, or can't get up in the morning, or for whom a malaise seems to set in.

As with all the other emotional reactions to being fired, the key to coping with them is to be aware of what is happening. Do the best you can to channel this energy into looking for a new job.

Shame and Embarrassment

That you should feel embarrassed is not all that surprising. After all, people who get fired usually deserve it, right? In fact, they often do, but just as often they don't. And even if you "deserved it" in some abstract sense, because your heart wasn't in your work or because you should have seen it coming long ago, this doesn't make you feel one iota better.

The fact is that it's embarrassing to be fired. There's no getting around it. No matter how wrong the company may be, if it has singled you out for firing, then there is someone in that company who feels you have failed. If you are part of a major layoff, then you are part of a collective failure of some kind. This is embarrassing. Maybe it shouldn't be, but it is.

The important question to ask yourself here is a simple one: "So what?" People get fired every day. Most people get fired at least once in their lifetimes, and many get fired multiple times. They get fired for good reasons and for stupid ones. Furthermore, we all find ways of embarrassing ourselves every day, and we survive just the same.

Is it awkward to be out of work? Yes, it is. Is it uncomfortable to ask your friends and business acquaintances for employment ideas? Absolutely. Do you have any option to being in this situation? For the moment, the answer obviously is no. So push past it.

There are lots of other emotions that people may feel. Some are thrilled to be out from under a terrible boss or a terrible company or to be finally released from the tormenting fear of being fired that was building over time. Some feel guilt over putting their families through the travails of unemployment. Some feel the sadness of a loss of connection and relationships. In fact, every major emotion may be experienced, depending on the circumstances.

What you need to do is to set your sights forward. I don't mean that you should ignore your emotions; in fact, if you ignore them, they are certain to leak out later at some inconvenient time. And you learn very little from the hard knocks in life unless you experience the emotions that go with them. What I mean is that you must be aware of your emotions, examine them carefully, and deal with them individually as best you can.

In my experience, the best way to deal with them, in addition to talking about them with people you trust, is to develop a plan. Start by developing a routine that will keep structure in your life. Until yesterday you were getting up every morning, going to work for a bunch of hours, coming home at the end of the day, and generally following a life pattern. The worst thing that can happen to you is to be without a pattern. Since no one is going to create it for you at this moment, you're going to have to create it for yourself.

Treat job hunting as a job. Get up early each morning, get dressed as if for work, and consider yourself employed. Your new employment responsibility is to find yourself a job. This takes eight to ten hours a day, every weekday. It takes hundreds of phone calls, thousands of résumés, lots of embarrassing approaches to old friends and business acquaintances. This book is not about searching for a job, but I have one simple piece of advice relevant to that: Set yourself specific objectives for each day and don't stop work for the day until you have achieved them. It might be some number of phone calls made, some number of interviews arranged, a pile of résumés mailed, or . . . you name it. *Treat the job search as a job.*

As part of this pattern, be sure to set aside some time for reflection. Sometimes people get fired because they are engaged in an activity for which they have no enthusiasm, which in turn gets reflected in their work. As you are unemployed anyway, now is the time to consider whether a different career direction is in order. But agonizing over this for hours at a time is unproductive and even counterproductive. My philosophy on the job search and on overcoming the trauma of job loss is very simple: The best way to start is to start.

Chapter 9

Is the Law on Your Side?

This book is not a substitute for a competent attorney. It is not even intended to be a comprehensive book on the subject of employment law, of which there are several (my personal favorite of those suitable for the layman being *Every Employee's Guide to the Law* by Lewin G. Joel III). However, you should understand the basics of the law to start thinking about whether you need an attorney; that is the purpose of this chapter and much of the rest of this book. Keep in mind that the focus in every instance will be on employment law *as it relates to terminations*.

A question that is frequently asked is where to find an attorney who actually understands employment law. Fortunately, this question is easy to answer. The National Employment Lawyers Association (NELA) is the national association of attorneys who represent employees and ex-employees in employment law cases. NELA was founded in 1985 and lists over 2,000 attorneys around the country as specialists in the field. If you want a referral to such experts in your area, send a self-addressed stamped envelope to NELA, 600 Harrison Street, San Francisco, California 94107.

The most relevant concept in the law dealing with termination issues is that of "at-will employment." If you do not have a written employment contract, which most of us do not, you are an "at-will" employee. In simple terms, this means that you are employed for no specific period of time *at the will* of your employer; in other words, you can be fired at any time for any reason that does not violate the law. It also means that you are free to quit at any time for any reason. In virtually every state, the courts will presume that you are an at-will employee unless you have an agreement with your employer to the contrary.

Now, if it seems to you that your rights as an employee under this doctrine are weaker than those of your employer, you are absolutely right. The rise of the "at-will" concept was little more than the power of employers exerted in the courts to establish that they can fire you whenever they want to. Other than in conditions of indentured servitude or slavery, there has never really been any obstacle to quitting a job, so the "at-will" doctrine has given employees very little.

Fortunately for you, employers in the past have occasionally abused this right so flagrantly that the courts have started to take notice and begun to recognize that there are certain circumstances under which firing is unfair and in some cases illegal.

No federal law focuses specifically on rules regarding the firing of employees. But a variety of laws prevent employment discrimination based on race, age, sex, and other criteria, and these laws include prohibitions on termination. There are also a variety of federal laws that prohibit retaliation (including firing) against employees who report violations of these laws. In recent years the National Conference of Commissioners on Uniform State Law has made an effort to draft a uniform employment termination act that in turn could be adopted by the individual states, but these efforts have come to naught. So far, only one state (Montana) has a law on the books dealing with this subject (see Appendix I and II), although others have such laws in the works. As a result, in most termination situations, the courts must examine these issues on a one-at-a-time basis.

A variety of doctrines or concepts are recognized by the courts as legitimate bases for bringing suit over termination. These typically are lumped under the heading of "wrongful discharge" suits. What this means is that you are claiming that you have been discharged for a wrongful reason, and that you are seeking redress in the courts. Four such doctrines recognized by a substantial number of courts are worth discussing in detail.

Violation of Law or Public Policy

Although it may seem obvious, your employer may not fire you in violation of existing law. This type of prohibition takes one of two forms: the anti-discrimination protections and your right to pursue certain activities.

First, there are federal and state antidiscrimination laws on the books. These are detailed in Chapter 11 and Appendix I. In general, you may not be fired for reasons of race, sex, age, national origin, religion, or your physical or mental disability. In certain states, you are also protected as to sexual preference, arrest record, and marital status, and occasionally yet other criteria are applied.

It is interesting that when these discrimination laws were written, mostly in the 1960s and 1970s, the emphasis seemed to be on hiring and promotion practices. That is because they were written during relatively good economic times. In recent years, however, with companies retrenching and reducing staffs, much of the effort has gone into evaluating dismissals for discriminatory content. At least 80 percent of current discrimination suits relate in one way or another to the discharge process.

However, there are other public policy issues as well. For example, in many states you cannot be fired for missing work because of serving on a jury. You often cannot be fired for complaining about company policies that you feel violate the law. You typically cannot be fired for meeting your military reserve obligation. You cannot be fired for participating in legitimate union organizing activities or for filing workers' compensation claims. You typically cannot be fired for refusing to break the law when requested to do so by your employer or for refusing to perjure yourself on your employer's behalf. Again, keep in mind that these are state-level prohibitions; federal law takes no position on these subjects except in a few specialized situations.

A subset of this doctrine is known as the "whistle-blower" protection. What this means is that you are entitled to point out violations of the law to your employer, and to report these violations to the appropriate state or federal authorities, without fear of being fired. In some states you are required to report violations to your employer first to get this protection.

A typical example of blowing the whistle is complaining about a health or safety hazard or about discriminatory employment practices.

The potential whistle-blower needs to be cautious. Laws differ from state to state. In many states only state or public employees are protected under existing statutes, although there may be specific coverage for employees of certain types of private employers. Administrative remedies are typically available through state agencies, and there may be very precise rules as to the sequence of events you must follow if you are to protect yourself. It can also be difficult to determine in advance if a law really has been violated.

Generally, it is not essential that a law actually have been violated for you to be protected for blowing the whistle. Most courts have held that you are protected if you have registered a complaint in good faith, believing that a law has been broken. This obviously is a subjective line that must be drawn.

Perhaps more important, notwithstanding the law and the courts, whistle-blowers are not exactly popular with their employers. Almost certainly you will be seen as a traitor, and even your co-workers may object to your behavior. For this reason, it is very important that you think carefully before blowing the whistle. In general, you should be prepared to be fired or at best bumped off your career path if you decide to blow the whistle, regardless of the law in your state. Thus you must weigh issues of public safety, personal and co-worker safety, personal and public ethics, and your own career interests all at the same time. Only you can determine which of these should prevail.

Nevertheless, if you do decide to blow the whistle, doing so is theoretically protected in many instances; see Appendix I for details.

Violation of a Nonwritten or Implied Contract

Most people do not have written employment contracts. However, employers sometimes say or do things that imply a contractual or long-term relationship. If the fired employee can establish the promise of such a relationship, legal action may be productive when termination occurs.

The simplest form of implied contract derives from words in the printed employee manual. Most companies have grown more sophisticated in recent years, but it still is not unusual to find employee handbooks that virtually guarantee lifetime employment. To see if this might apply to you, you should look for statements like the following:

- A statement that you as an employee will keep your job as long as you perform to a certain standard.
- A statement that an employee will be terminated only "for cause," which implies some gross violation of acceptable behavior. It is especially useful if "cause" is defined; typically it will involve such transgressions as willful misconduct or theft. If the company specifically lays out reasons why someone can be fired, and does not make it clear that there are many other reasons for being fired that are not specifically cited, you may

have cause for legal action if you were fired without having violated any of the specific prohibitions listed.
- A statement that employees are regarded as "permanent" after some probationary period or after the completion of a training program.
- A statement that you can be fired for any reason or for no reason at all during the probationary period. Some courts have interpreted this kind of phrasing to imply that you have thereby been given a guarantee of not being fired once the probationary period has ended.
- A statement that you are entitled to some kind of process when there are problems. This might be a guarantee of a specific set of disciplinary procedures or of performance evaluations. The question in this case is whether or not these procedures were followed before you were terminated.
- A statement expressing the company's sense of pride that bad economic times in the past have not resulted in employee layoffs.
- A statement that the company strives for a culture in which the employees regard themselves as one happy family and in which the company strives for success and continued employment for all.

In an effort to reduce litigation risks, many companies now insert a paragraph in their employee handbooks stating that nothing contained in the handbook should be construed as a guarantee of employment and that all employees are "at-will" employees, free to quit or be fired at any time. These clauses offer some protection to the company, but courts in a variety of states have upheld wrongful discharge claims when other paragraphs in the handbook implied a guarantee of employment.

One event to watch out for is the issuance of a new employee handbook. As companies become more sophisticated, they will reword their handbooks to make the at-will employment issue clearer. However, some courts have taken the position that such a change, from wording that does not emphasize the at-will relationship to wording that does, constitutes a change in the employment relationship that requires "consideration"; that is, you should get something for giving up these rights. Unfortunately, no one has ever determined what that something should be. What is essential is that you keep the handbook that was in use when you were hired and any new versions that have been issued subsequently.

Statements that may affect your employment relationship are made even more often by managers during the hiring or performance evaluation process. Although companies may have gotten much more sophisticated about the wording in their employee handbooks, it is much harder to control a supervisor who is trying to get someone hired or to keep someone happy. Here are some specific examples of the legal ramifications of statements by supervisors that have been used as the basis for wrongful discharge lawsuits:

- A court ruled that statements made by a supervisor in annual reviews to the effect that "I am glad you work here and hope we will have many more years working together" and that he "desired a long-term working relationship" with the employee could have created an employment contract.
- Because an employee was told that he would be promoted within six months of starting a job and that he would receive an annual salary and a specific vacation period, the employee was entitled to have a jury decide whether those statements created an employment contract for a specified period of time.
- Statements that an employee could expect job security as long as he did his job and that he could expect a promotion if he did a good job were deemed evidence that a contract of employment was created.
- A statement in an interview that potential employees did not have to worry about their jobs "as long as the job gets done" could be evidence of an offer of permanent employment.
- An employee used his supervisor's statement that "we will retire together" to allege in court that he had a lifetime employment contract.

These five examples all come from *Employee Termination Manual for Managers and Supervisors,* published in 1991 by Commerce Clearing House.* It provides an excellent short summary of termination issues from the employer's point of view.

The key point here is that supervisors are perceived by employees to speak for the company, and employees assume (correctly, from a legal point of view) that they should treat a supervisor's comments as if they represented the company's position on a given issue.

*Reproduced with permission from *Employee Termination Manual for Managers and Supervisors.* Published and copyrighted by Commerce Clearing House, Inc., 4025 W. Paterson Ave., Chicago, Illinois 60646.

An important legal principle regarding such oral contracts is found in the Statute of Frauds, a law dating back to seventeenth-century England. Most states have some version of it. In general, these statutes require that agreements be in writing to be enforceable, and that oral agreements must be able to be dispatched (that is, carried out) within one year to be enforceable. As a result, an oral agreement to employ you for more than a year is difficult to enforce in some states even if both sides agree that the oral agreement was made.

In many states, however, the principle that is applied by the courts is that it must be "possible" to enforce the agreement within one year. As it almost always is possible, even if not likely (for example, you could die or the company could go out of business), these kinds of contracts often are enforceable. This is one of those areas where you should consult a lawyer.

Finally, many courts are prepared to assume an implied contract from other things your employer has done. This is an even fuzzier notion in that it does not hinge on specific written or oral statements, but it nevertheless can be very powerful. The concept essentially is as follows: You have been treated as a productive, successful employee over an extended period of time. Even if you have been made no specific promises about employment, such promises are inherent in your employer's behavior and thus it is unreasonable for your employer to fire you.

Here are some of the factors a court might consider:

- Your tenure with the company (how long you have worked there)
- The quality of your performance evaluations
- The lack of negative performance evaluations or of any performance evaluations at all
- The rate at which you have been promoted
- The recognition you have received (for example, sales awards or Employee of the Month kudos)
- Whether you were recruited away from other stable employment
- Statements regarding stable or permanent employment made to other employees, even if such statements were never made to you.

The point to all this is that employers are caught on the horns of a dilemma: They want to be able to fire you when they want to, but they don't want to make you so nervous about it that you quit before they are ready to have you leave. The company's legal department wants employee handbooks that read like contracts, while the human resources department wants them to be friendly documents with a minimum of threatening or legal language. It is in this disjunction that the implied contract concept arises.

The Covenant of Good Faith and Fair Dealing

The covenant concept arose originally from the relationship between insurance companies and the individual insured. The idea is that individuals are entitled to reasonable treatment independent of any specific contract or violation of law. If this notion sounds hard to define, that is because it is. The courts, if they are willing to consider the concept at all, generally look for some specific behavior on the part of the employer that a reasonable person would find offensive. For example, if you were misled about your future opportunities to advance, or to get raises, or to be transferred into a different job category or to a different location, this could imply a breach of good faith or fair dealing.

What is difficult here is to define what was said or implied and what interpretation it should have been given. If your employer told you that if you took a specific assignment you would be considered for a transfer to another department, and that everyone else who had taken that assignment previously had gotten that transfer, then it would not be surprising if a court regarded your employer as having guaranteed you such a transfer. On the other hand, if you were merely told that a certain kind of training was a prerequisite to being considered for a transfer, but that no transfer was guaranteed, and that in fact there were six applicants for every opening in that other department, your failure to get the transfer is not likely to be interpreted as a breach of good faith or fair dealing.

In general, you will not be able to rely on the Covenant of Good Faith and Fair Dealing by itself. It is most useful when combined with an implied contract dispute or a public policy issue. Your attorney, if you have one, will try hard to get the judge to accept the principle and to have the judge instruct the jury to consider it, but many judges will refuse to go along.

As you can see, this is a difficult area of the "at-will" doctrine. Precisely for this reason, it is the most perilous area for employers in that there are no easy guidelines for them to follow. The courts have recognized this by making the burden of proof on you quite considerable, and in many states the courts have completely rejected this concept as the basis for wrongful discharge lawsuits. Even California, which had taken the lead in acceptance of this principle in the courts, took a big step backward in the now-famous 1988 Foley case, and today it is much more difficult to sell the good faith and fair dealing principle to a California court.

Other examples that might be considered violations of this covenant include lying to or misleading you about the dangers of a specific job as an inducement to get you to take it; transferring you to avoid paying you some bonus or commission; firing you for what are stated to be performance reasons when the real reasons are something else (for example, to replace you with someone who earns less or to avoid fulfilling some other promise made to you); and deliberately treating you badly to force you to quit so that severance pay will not be required. As you can see, all these claims are difficult to prove.

Defamation

Defamation is the act of making false statements about someone that damage that person. Other words used to describe this act are slander (defamation by spoken word) or libel (defamation by written word). A common definition is that defamation occurs if an employer "publishes" (speaks or writes) a false statement about an employee that harms the employee's reputation and that becomes known to people who should not know it.

In the context of terminations, defamation is a tricky principle. First of all, it can rarely be used to challenge a firing. By its nature, defamation is something that happens after the fact, typically in reference checking or in conversations between supervisors and employees at the company from which you have been fired. As a result, it is not an effective vehicle for reinstatement to your position or for wrongful discharge suits in general, and the legal community typically does not lump it in with other examples of exceptions to at-will employment.

Second, defamation is extremely difficult to prove. It is hard to find out that it even took place, and it is based on the recollections of others as to spoken words; rarely is there a defamation case about written communication. Furthermore, it hinges on truth; that is, you have not been defamed if the words spoken or written were true, unless you can show—which is also extremely difficult—that the information transmitted was so damaging and so maliciously delivered and so intended to damage that the truth of it will be ignored by a court.

Employers have become quite sophisticated about defending themselves against defamation lawsuits. Any and all of the following defenses will work in some cases: The information is true (this is the strongest defense); the information is not damaging; the information was provided in good faith; the information was limited to the specific inquiry; the information was disclosed at the proper time and in the proper manner (that is, not to the wrong people and not in public); the person seeking the information had a legitimate business need for it.

The law in this area too has changed over time. For example, it used to be accepted that employers were liable for false statements under all circumstances. This meant that no matter how careful the employer was to establish that a statement (such as in a reference check) was true, there was liability if the statement later turned out to be false. In 1974, however, the U.S. Supreme Court narrowed this concept, making employers liable for a false statement only if they were negligent in attempting to make sure that the statement was true.

So if the fact of defamation is so tricky to prove, what is its usefulness? First of all, it is a means of collecting monetary compensation in situations where you may have been fired for legitimate reasons (that is, you have no claims based on a violation of public policy, the breaking of an implied contract, or dealing in bad faith). But even if you were fired legitimately for performance or other reasons, your employer cannot lie about the facts or willfully attempt to sully your reputation. If he does so, not matter how legal and fair your firing was, he is defaming you.

Second, unlike many termination situations, defamation falls under the category of tort law. A tort is an intentional or careless act that directly harms someone. What this means is that you can collect punitive damages, or damages in addition to your specific costs and losses ("punitive" simply means that your ex-company is being punished for its actions), and damages for emotional suffering.

Punitive damages are based not on the size of the damage done to you but on an assessment of how big an award will make your former employer feel pain. In many termination litigation efforts, the most you can accomplish is to get your job back with back pay or some modest amount of reimbursement while you are looking for a new job, so entering the world of tort law can have considerable financial implications. A breach of good faith lawsuit also comes under tort law in some cases.

In isolated cases, the results of defamation lawsuits have been spectacular. In 1993, Procter & Gamble was hit with a $15.6 million judgment ($1.6 million in actual damages and $14 million in punitive damages) for posting notices on company bulletin boards saying that a long-term employee had been fired for stealing a telephone. In another case, a former Contel executive who had been criticized in public by Contel employees both before and after he was fired won a $3.5 million judgment that was later increased to $7.1 million. In both cases, the appeals process will probably go on for years, but the possible results are extraordinary.

The downside is that a defamation lawsuit may result in the spreading of information about you which for now may be relatively contained but which, even if untrue, is embarrassing and perhaps believable to some people who don't know all the facts.

A special case within the defamation category is that of blacklisting. This is a situation in which an employer, or in some cases a union, goes out of its way to prevent you from getting new employment. There have been cases where unions have distributed lists of people who are tagged "unacceptable" and who therefore should not be sent out on jobs. More commonly, employers have discreetly or not so discreetly warned potential employers away from specific individuals.

There are ways you can protect yourself against this practice and ways to find out if it is going on. These are discussed in Chapter 7. The states that have specific antiblacklisting legislation are listed in Appendix I.

In general, defamation as a basis for litigation is the last resort. Although there have been some spectacular financial windfalls from these suits, the settlements typically are not large (averaging about $60,000, according to one source) and they are hard to get.

Chapter 10

Should You Sue?

It is not the premise of this book that lawsuits are a good idea, but neither do I believe categorically that they are a bad idea. The real way to win in termination situations is to be prepared before the fact to derail the termination process before it occurs and to respond to it with knowledge and negotiating ability if there is no way that the termination can be prevented. Many potentially litigious situations can be avoided by advance preparation, and it is the need for this preparation that is the driving force behind this book.

However, you may well be reading this book from the vantage point of having already been fired and wanting to know what you can do about it. The specifics of the laws are contained in the appendixes. The question here is whether lawsuits in general are a good idea.

First of all, keep in mind that the word *lawsuit* may have two different meanings in the case of terminations. You can file a complaint with the Equal Employment Opportunity Commission (EEOC) or its equivalent state agencies (see Chapter 11 and Appendix I) if you have been discriminated against or in most cases of terminations that are in violation of public policy. This sort of filing is not in the usual sense a lawsuit, because you do not need a lawyer and because no judges or traditional courtrooms are involved.

Unfortunately, because of unbelievable caseloads, the EEOC and comparable state agencies rarely get much for you. Small settlements (under $15,000) are reasonably common, but many complaints are dismissed entirely, and rarely does the whole process carry through to a favorable finding and a meaningful financial victory.

Alternatively, you can file a regular lawsuit with an attorney. If you have an employment discrimination situation, this can occur only after you have exhausted your administrative alternatives with the EEOC or other agency (see Chapter 11 for details). In this chapter, *lawsuit* should be assumed to cover both types of action unless otherwise specified.

So, to return to the original question: Are lawsuits a good idea? There is a simple answer to this question: maybe. It depends on the circumstances and on your appetite for aggravation and spending money. You must keep in mind a few salient facts.

1. *Wrongful discharge suits are hard to win.* Like it or not, unfair or not, the at-will employment doctrine is well supported by over a hundred years of litigation. It is weaker than it used to be, and it shows signs of getting weaker still, but in the vast majority of situations the simple truth is that your employer has the right to fire you.

Yes, there are exceptions, and you may be one of them. But do not be deceived by your sense of moral indignation or by the stories you read in the newspaper about large settlements. These settlements are news in part because of their size and in part because they are a deviation from normal practice; normal practice is that, within certain boundaries, your employer can fire you for any reason whatsoever or for no reason at all.

It is hard to get statistics on the difficulty of winning wrongful discharge suits. Most of what I have seen suggests that something under 20 percent of these suits are successful. The problem with these statistics, of course, is that companies often settle out of court or even before a lawsuit is filed so as to avoid lengthy litigation. Lewin Joel, in *Every Employee's Guide to the Law,* says that the average cost for a company to defend itself against such a lawsuit is $80,000, win or lose.

In any event, keep in mind that you are engaging in an uphill battle. The desire for revenge can run strong, and it is this desire that prompts many such suits, but the ferocity of your feelings will have little to do with the outcome.

2. *Wrongful termination suits can be expensive.* Unless you can assemble a class-action suit (one in which you and many other people file suit together, or in which you file suit on behalf of a much larger group of people, as in a major layoff), it can be difficult to get a contingency attorney to take your side. (A contingency attorney is one to whom you pay nothing and who collects his or her fee as a percentage of the proceeds won in court.)

Most attorneys know full well that these are hard cases to win, and that the settlements tend to be modest unless the case falls under tort law (as described in Chapter 9). Tort law allows for punitive damages as well as damages for emotional suffering, but the bulk of wrongful discharge cases do not qualify for this.

As a result, you will probably have to retain an attorney who will charge you hourly, and legal bills can easily exceed $10,000 and in some cases much more. On the other hand, many of the attorneys who are members of the National Employment Lawyers Association will accept some contingency element in their fee, and there is some trend to an increasing contingency portion in these kinds of cases. Just keep in mind that whatever money you pay on an hourly basis will be entirely at risk; if you lose in court, the money is gone. Filing with the EEOC, by contrast, is free, so expense is irrelevant in those cases. However, those cases often turn into lawsuits later; in any event, with the EEOC you may get exactly what you pay for.

3. *You may have signed away your right to sue.* I have discussed at length the arguments for and against signing "waiver to sue" documents. The fact that you have signed one of these does not make a lawsuit impossible, but it does mean that it will be very difficult to get an attorney to take your case. Judges like settlements, and a waiver to sue agreement is essentially the same as a settlement. The fact that you have actively considered and discussed with your employer the idea of a lawsuit and then signed a document saying that you will not sue in exchange for some quid pro quo (that is, some type of extra compensation) will make it that much more difficult to win in court. The fact that you have a legitimate claim may get subordinated to the fact that you can be viewed as having signed a binding contract.

4. *Your life will become an open book.* This is one of the primary arguments against suing. Your past employer almost certainly has more resources than you do. These resources can be used to gather information about you. They can be used to interview your neighbors, to examine your driving and police records, to gather information from your health and life insurance companies, to gather data from your past co-workers, and potentially to embarrass you in myriad ways. Your ex-employer has easy access to all your past supervisors, peers, and subordinates, and also has a great deal of leverage on any of them who still work for the company.

You must assume that it is possible that anything in your past will come out in court. Theoretically, the judge will not allow the introduction of personal issues that are irrelevant to the case. However, as an example, if you were fired for excessive tardiness, your employer will dig deep to find the reason for that tardiness. Did you tend to stay out drinking at night and then have trouble getting up in the morning to go to work? That will become public information. Were you having an affair in the morning before work and arriving late as a result? That will become public too. Were you leaving home on time and doing anything on the way to work, no matter how trivial, that would be embarrassing to you? Prepare to be embarrassed.

Furthermore, every tiny failing at work will be discussed. No one is a perfect employee. Even if you were one of the best, there will be people who don't like you, people who feel that you did a poor job on something, people who feel that they should have gotten the promotion you got. Even if your attorney manages to keep your outside personal life out of the process, your work life with all its little failings will be discussed openly. Do you have the backbone for this?

5. *You need lots of documentation.* Filing a lawsuit is easy, but having the necessary information to win one is something else. Were you keeping a log at work? Can you obtain statements from your co-workers that support your claims? Do you know what is in your personnel file? Some of these materials are available after the lawsuit is filed, but you need to have the sense that there is information to be gathered.

Your former co-workers still work for your former employer. They may be reluctant to come forward, and with good reason. In fact, in a perverse kind of way, if your former company really has stepped over the line in firing you and is known to be the kind of employer that engages in this type of behavior, this may make your former co-workers even less likely to participate in your case. You should consider this intimidation factor.

6. *Cases like this can be enormously time-consuming.* In fact, one of the strategies used by companies when they are sued by individuals is to take enormously lengthy depositions. These are meetings in which the company's lawyer questions you in the presence of your lawyer, and they have been known to go on for days. This is not only a time issue; if you are paying your attorney by the hour, the meter is ticking while the depositions drone on. You can add to this the time you spend observing your lawyer's depositions of your former employer, the time you spend just talking with your own lawyer, the time you spend doing research, and the time you spend in court.

Fortunately, new federal rules make long depositions harder to justify, so in most cases they will be limited to a day or two. But you have to be there for these, so be prepared to take the time. You may have limitless time. On the other hand, if you are unemployed you should be spending the bulk of your time looking for a job. If you have found new employment, your new employer is certainly not going to be thrilled about giving you time off right after you have started work—and even less so for the purpose of suing a former employer. Be sure to ask your attorney how much of *your* time will be required.

7. *Potential new employers will be very reluctant to hire you if they know you are in the midst of litigation with your former employer, or even if they know that you have initiated such litigation in the past.* If you have already started a new job, your new employer will equally be less than thrilled.

People who file lawsuits are seen as litigious and as trouble-makers. No company wants to be sued, and there is no effective law preventing a company from refusing to hire you for having filed a lawsuit. Title VII of the Civil Rights Act (Title VII) supposedly protects people who file complaints with the EEOC, but it is quite easy to get around this prohibition. In virtually every instance, employers who learn that a prospective employee is in the midst of wrongful discharge litigation with a former employer will refuse to hire that person.

To some extent, this is an irrational decision. After all, your firing may have been a gross injustice and you may be absolutely right in your decision to sue; this is a free country, isn't it? And the fact that another employer treated you inappropriately and you sued as a result should be irrelevant if your new employer plans to treat you fairly.

On the other hand, this lawsuit will take time, and no employer wants an employee who is already obligated to take time off. This is what the company will say if it says anything at all. The larger truth is that companies just don't like employees who have any tendency to sue, and especially if they are suing their employers. Rather than having to contemplate any such aggravation, they pass. Therefore, as a simple rule of thumb, get a new job before filing a lawsuit, don't tell your prospective employers that you are going to file one or have filed one, and if you need to take any days off for depositions or court appearances, take vacation days and don't tell anyone where you are.

So it isn't easy. But that doesn't mean that you never should sue.

First of all, you may genuinely have been wronged and been meaningfully damaged. If you are of an age that makes getting a new senior position very difficult in spite of the age discrimination laws, or if you have lost major retirement benefits or bonuses, the lawsuit may be worth it. If you feel you must clear your name in some way, the same may be true. If you are planning to retire anyway, and thus have time available and aren't worried about a new employer, the negatives are mitigated considerably.

And there can be wonderful outcomes. The Commerce Clearing House claims that the average settlement in wrongful termination suits that are won by the ex-employee is $600,000, and it cites examples of settlements that go well into the millions. A survey of 515 trial verdicts from 1988 to 1992 reports that age discrimination suits resulted in an average award of $302,914, sex discrimination awards averaged $255,734, race discrimination awards averaged $176,578, and disability discrimination awards averaged $151,241. Yet another study showed that the average wrongful termination jury award in California in 1992 was $1.3 million, several times higher than a few years earlier!

These averages are very misleading, however. They include only those cases that actually went to court (that is, not settlements negotiated by the EEOC or a state agency, as discussed in Chapter 11 and Appendix I) and exclude the many cases that never make it as far as a courtroom. The average settlement of all claims (including many in which there is no settlement at all) is much lower.

Many companies will settle rather than go through the time, cost, and risk of litigation. There have been cases in which one call from a lawyer was enough to result in cash paid. But you shouldn't count on this. Really big settlements require that punitive damages apply, which often they do not, and companies are getting experienced at these kinds of lawsuits.

The point here is that lawsuits are serious, expensive, time-consuming, and often debilitating. They should not be entered into lightly. You should not assume that you will get a sympathetic hearing, nor that the law is on your side just because you are an individual fighting a corporation. If you are serious about suing, you should take the time to find a lawyer who has real experience in at-will litigation and then listen carefully to what he or she tells you about the odds and likely financial outcome. Only if it still makes business and personal sense should you proceed.

Chapter 11

Firing and the Federal Laws

All of our lives are covered by a long list of federal laws, and many of these relate to employment: discrimination laws, wage and hour laws, safety laws. The wording of the laws alone occupies thousands of pages, and the books written on the interpretation of these laws and the cases that deal with them would fill a small metropolitan library.

Notwithstanding this long-term outburst of enthusiasm by the lawmakers, there is not one single law that makes it illegal to fire someone. Nevertheless, many laws do constrain the specific circumstances under which firing can take place, and offer redress and damages in certain circumstances. This chapter is focused on those laws. (There are also many state laws relating to employment, some of which are more restrictive or more generous than comparable federal laws. Be sure to read the section of Appendix I that refers to the state in which you work.)

Keep in mind that every federal law listed here is much broader in scope than the firing issue. In fact, in some cases the issue of employee termination occupies but a few sentences or paragraphs in a law that fills fifty or a hundred pages. What I have tried to do is extract the portions relevant to the topic at hand.

Title VII of the Civil Rights Act of 1964 (Title VII), as Amended by the 1991 Civil Rights Act

These two statutes in combination are the current foundation for the prevention of discrimination in employment in the United States. They are among the most controversial laws ever passed; indeed, the

1991 law was passed largely to defuse a variety of U.S. Supreme Court decisions that had whittled away at the provisions of Title VII.

In simple terms, these laws make it illegal for a private employer or local or state government (not the federal government) to discriminate against employees on the basis of race, skin color, national origin, religious beliefs, or gender (the sex of the individual). Pregnancy as a discrimination factor also was added in 1978, and there is proposed legislation to add sexual orientation to the list of protected categories.

As relates to being fired, these laws state that none of the criteria listed above may be considered by an employer when terminating someone. This means that you may not be fired because of your race, gender, and so forth. It also means that any indication that people of a particular protected group are fired more frequently than others may be a cause for legal action.

As you can imagine, the arguments on this subject are fierce. If you are of Chinese extraction, and I fire you for what I consider your poor performance, and I am known to dislike Chinese people, does this prove that you were discriminated against? If I fire you for trying to convert your fellow employees to the Mormon faith, even though you engaged in this activity only at lunchtime in the cafeteria, have I violated your religious rights? If I fire you, a woman, for insisting that you want to be a sports reporter with access to the men's football locker room, is this sex discrimination?

These and thousands of other similar questions have been posed in a variety of legal actions, and the answers are not simple ones. Each situation must be examined individually, and the results are by no means consistent.

Title VII created a mechanism for pursuing discrimination complaints: the Equal Employment Opportunity Commission (EEOC). If you feel you have been fired for discriminatory reasons, it is to the EEOC that you must turn first. In most states, the EEOC has designated what are known as "706 Agencies." These are governmental units, typically state, county, or city human rights commissions or their equivalent, to which the EEOC defers during the early stages of a complaint. In general, the EEOC will not act until you have first filed a complaint with the local 706 agency and sixty days have passed either with no action or your case has been terminated. Only then will the EEOC itself consider your complaint. In certain cases where the state has no equal employment regulations or exempts a particular form of discrimination, you can proceed directly to the EEOC without the sixty-day waiting period. The 706 agencies in each state are listed in Appendix I.

The EEOC rules are straightforward. You don't have to identify yourself by name, and the EEOC will try to keep your name secret— but don't count on it. To get this secrecy, ideally you should have a third party file on your behalf, but your name must be provided so that the EEOC can contact you for investigatory purposes.

You must file your complaint at an EEOC office or at its designated local agency (typically called a Fair Employment Practices Agency) within 180 days of the event you feel was discriminatory, in this case a termination. If you file with a state agency first, you have 300 days from the date of the alleged unlawful discrimination to file with the EEOC, or thirty days after the state terminates its proceedings, whichever is sooner. The EEOC then has 180 days to take action. If it fails to act in this 180-day period, you can get a right-to-sue letter from the EEOC entitling you to proceed to a normal lawsuit process, after which you then have ninety days to file suit.

This all sounds great. The problem is that the EEOC has an unbelievable backlog, and this backlog has been growing over the years. In 1994 about 95,000 charges alleging employment discrimination were filed with the EEOC. Many are the cases that get lost in the system or that simply cannot be processed in the required 180 days. In fact, the EEOC itself has stated that the average case in 1993 involved a 270-day wait. This is partly because of government bureaucracy and funding cuts. The typical EEOC investigator in 1994 was handling over 175 cases at any given moment, far too many by almost any standard and twice as many as were handled in 1990.

However, the backlog is also caused by the incredibly large number of people in our increasingly litigious society who want to "sue" their former employers. I put the word *sue* in quotation marks because filing a complaint with the EEOC is not in fact a lawsuit in that there are no judges and courtrooms involved. You reach the lawsuit stage only if you choose to do so after getting the right-to-sue letter described earlier.

The simple fact is that something like 70 percent of the U.S. population is covered by the antidiscrimination laws. Does this sound unbelievable? Just think of the categories. In fact, you could argue that 100 percent of us are covered, since we all have a gender or a national origin or fit into some other category. But even looking at the categories more narrowly, most of us could figure out a way to claim discrimination. White males file antidiscrimination lawsuits all the time. Christians claim to have been discriminated against by other religious groups. It is not necessary that you be part of a minority group to be discriminated against. So it is easy to see how the EEOC has become so overburdened.

Potential Disqualifiers

The question of whether you should go to the EEOC to protest a termination is a complex one. If you have the slightest doubt, at least visit an EEOC agency and talk about the criteria for the commission's support. Some of the potential disqualifiers are these:

Employers With Fewer than Fifteen Employees

These are not covered by the federal antidiscrimination laws. Strange as it may seem, if you work for a company with fewer than fifteen employees, it can fire you for discriminatory reasons and the EEOC will do nothing to help you. Some states cover smaller employers with their antidiscrimination laws; details on each state are in Appendix I.

Jobs With Bona Fide Occupational Qualifications (BFOQs)

This means that there is some legitimate reason for insisting that the people in these jobs have particular characteristics. For example, you can be refused a job as a religious counselor in a Buddhist organization if you are not a Buddhist. It is possible that you can be prevented from playing Queen Elizabeth in a play because you are a man. In very narrow circumstances, you can be prevented from being a security guard in an all-male prison because you are a woman. However, there are no BFOQs relating to race; that is, there is no job for which discrimination based on race is allowable.

Notice that most of these are hiring issues. Most people never find themselves in a situation where they are fired because of a BFOQ; the odds that you as a man have been playing Queen Elizabeth already and are fired because someone discovers that you are male are not very high. But you need to be aware that there are certain legitimate job requirements that may affect your employment.

This is a tricky area of the law. For example, would you imagine that someone could be fired because of lack of strength or physical stature? The qualification sounds legitimate enough for certain kinds of jobs. If you were going to work in a warehouse and needed to lift

100-pound bags of concrete all day long, doesn't it make sense that someone small or weak would be kept out of such a job? Maybe. But this qualification could have the effect of discriminating against women or against anyone from a nationality group whose members tend to be shorter or smaller than average. So whereas strength may be a BFOQ, its usage as a discrimination factor is very delicate.

Specific BFOQ-Related Issues

• *Gender.* In certain instances, discrimination based on gender is permissible if the job requires it (the BFOQ case) or if there is a "business necessity." These cases are interpreted very narrowly. The requirement that guards in an all-male prison be male was upheld, but it was a situation where the prison was understaffed, had dormitory-style sleeping arrangements, and had a high proportion of sex offenders. The actor-actress BFOQ also has its limitations; for example, Peter Pan was played on Broadway by a woman, so it would be difficult for a producer to claim that the role requires a man or boy for credibility even though the Peter Pan character is male.

The "business necessity" argument is, if anything, even more difficult to make. For example, it would be totally unacceptable to argue that "women are less stable," "a male image would be better for this job," "women have poor attendance records," "the work is too dangerous for women," "having women around would create a moral problem with the men (or with the men's wives)," "our customers prefer men," "we would have to build separate restroom facilities," or "women don't like working night shifts."

• *National Origin.* Title VII provides for a theoretical situation where there could be a bona fide occupational qualification based on national origin. However, none such has been found to be legitimate thus far. In fact, even such job requirements that might tend to discriminate against certain nationalities (for example, by requiring that employees be of a certain height) are virtually indefensible.

Under the "business necessity" rule, it is allowable that employees be required to speak English sufficiently free of any foreign accent that they can be understood by co-workers and customers. There can be no presumption, however, that persons of a particular national group cannot meet this requirement.

Even if the job task is by some measure "national" in origin, such as a tour leader who must speak Italian, the only legitimate requirement is language proficiency; a Japanese or an American whose Italian is of sufficient quality may not be discriminated against.

• *Religion.* Independent of the specific BFOQ rules, religious institutions and schools that are owned by a specific religious group and that are propagating their religion are allowed to require that employees be of that religion.

Beyond this exception, there are very few cases in which religious discrimination is allowed. Employers must bend over backwards, for example, to accommodate Sabbath rules (for example, not working on Saturdays for certain faiths) and religious dress habits (like the growing of beards), unless they interfere with safety or health, and to be reasonable regarding special religious holidays. There are, however, circumstances when an employer is simply unable to accommodate religious requirements, and in such cases will be permitted to discriminate, but these cases are few and far between.

Under Title VII, if you are successful with an EEOC claim, usually what you can hope for is getting your job back together with back pay. This is not a vehicle for major financial reward. The Civil Rights Act of 1991 created the possibility of both compensatory and punitive damages, but only in cases of intentional discrimination (in which case compensatory damages, as for pain and suffering, are available) or unlawful harassment, malice, or reckless indifference to the law (in which case punitive damages are available), and there are limits on the awards available for such damages based on the size of the employer:

15–100 employees:	$ 50,000 limit
101–200 employees:	$100,000 limit
201–500 employees:	$200,000 limit
501 or more:	$300,000 limit

For example, in the first EEOC lawsuit under the Americans with Disabilities Act (see the latter part of this chapter), a jury awarded a plaintiff $572,000 and had the award reduced to $222,000 because of the limits just cited.

To collect punitive damages, there also must be evidence of malice or reckless indifference to the victim's federally protected rights. In any event, these larger financial awards require litigation, not just an EEOC filing.

Finally, you must keep in mind that going to the EEOC has its dangers. It is supposedly illegal for you to get into trouble for turning to the EEOC. For example, your current employer cannot fire you for doing so. But in the real world, the simple fact is that filing these kinds of complaints can get you a reputation as a troublemaker. And it is not unusual for past employers to tell potential future ones that you sued them or turned to the EEOC. You must weigh the benefits of discrimination claims against the dangers to your reputation that they represent.

The Age Discrimination in Employment Act of 1967 (ADEA) and the Older Workers Benefit Protection Act (1991)

After a series of twists and turns, the essence of age discrimination legislation is that persons over 40 may not be discriminated against by employers with twenty or more employees. This probably is the most important antidiscrimination law in the subject area of employee termination.

In general, for example, it is unlawful to require someone to re-tire because of age. There have, however, been some narrow excep-tions: Bus drivers, police officers, and pilots, for example, have in some cases been required to retire (or have not been hired) at age 60 for reasons related to safety. In fact, commercial airline pilots and copilots are required to retire at 60 under Federal Aviation Adminis-tration rules. It has been upheld that judges may be required to retire at age 70. There is also a special provision in the ADEA that senior-level executives and policy-making officials may be required to retire at age 65 if they would receive pensions and other ongoing compen-sation totaling at least $44,000 annually (in certain states a $27,000 guideline is used).

For a long time, the U.S. Supreme Court chipped away at ADEA in the area of benefit plans, holding that older employees could be discriminated against when it came to employee benefit plans like health insurance and pensions. This concept was overthrown by the Older Workers Benefit Protection Act, which specifically prohibits benefit plans from discriminating on the basis of age.

As regards termination practices, age is the biggest problem among all those that are discussed in this chapter. For years, it was a staple cost-cutting move in organizations to fire higher-paid people and to replace them with lower-paid ones, which effectively meant that older employees were replaced by younger ones. Rarely in the past was this action even slightly related to performance; indeed, it was often the case that employees who were performing fine were being replaced by learners.

After the passage of the ADEA, which quite clearly outlawed

these practices, employers began to adopt a different tactic: They would induce the older employee to sign a waiver of his or her legal rights in return for something, typically money. You will recall the long discussion of the "waiver of the right to sue" in Chapter 10. This was done under onerous circumstances or under subtle threat: Sign this waiver in exchange for these (paltry) benefits or we can't guarantee that we will offer you these benefits the next time we have a layoff. This is what was known as the "sign or starve" technique.

The Older Workers Benefit Protection Act went a long way toward eliminating this practice. What now is required of the employer is the following:

- The waiver must be in writing and must be written in a way so as to be understandable to the employee signing it.
- The waiver must make specific references to rights and claims of the ADEA and make it clear that the individual is waiving these rights and claims.
- The waiver does not eliminate any rights or claims that may arise after the date of the agreement.
- In exchange for the waiver, the individual must receive something to which he or she would not otherwise have been entitled.
- The employee must be advised in writing to consult an attorney about the signing and provisions of the waiver before signing it.
- The employee is given twenty-one days to consider the waiver (longer if an entire group of people is being asked to sign such a waiver) and the right to revoke his or her signature within seven days after signing.

The upshot of all this is that discrimination based on age has become much more difficult for employers. If you feel you have been discriminated against, your remedy still is with the EEOC, following basically the same rules outlined earlier in this chapter.

The Worker Adjustment and Retraining Notification Act of 1989

This statute, known as WARN, addresses the case of large employee layoffs. Specifically, it says that employers of 100 or more employees who intend to close a facility or engage in a mass layoff (defined as fifty or more people in a thirty-day period) must give sixty days' written notice to those employees and to the officials in the community where the facility is located.

Note that this is not a severance pay requirement; it does not mean that you can quit work on the day of the notice and continue to get paid for sixty days while you are looking for a new job. It merely means that you get sixty days of warning.

There are a number of exceptions to WARN. These include companies with fewer than 100 employees, certain large facilities where less than one-third of the work force is affected (even if it has more than fifty employees), part-time employees, layoffs caused by natural disasters or truly unforeseeable circumstances, temporary projects that were known to be temporary when the employees signed on, cases where the employer offers severance in lieu of notice, and cases where the employer offers new jobs within a reasonable commuting distance. In other words, there are a lot of exceptions.

Unfortunately, the implications of this and of lax enforcement, at least through the early 1990s, has been that plant closings and layoffs are resulting in no more advance warning being given to employees than before WARN was passed. Even with the many state laws on this subject (see Appendix I), there are very few cases in which employees are given meaningful advance notice.

If you feel that your WARN rights have been violated, you are entitled to sue and may under some circumstances receive up to three years' back pay and benefits. The company may also be subject to fines payable to the community in which it does business.

Americans with Disabilities Act of 1990 (ADA)

Under this statute, employers of more than fifteen employees may not discriminate against disabled persons. The basic rule is that a disabled employee must be eligible for hire and cannot be fired as long as he or she can perform the "essential functions" of the job with "reasonable accommodation" by the employer, presuming that the employer does not have to incur "undue hardship."

The secret to this law is the complexity in defining those phrases, and the law is new enough so that those definitions are still under legal review. For example, the definition of "undue hardship" for a large and wealthy employer would be different than it is for a small, struggling employer. Also, "undue hardship" can be construed to include situations that would disrupt the business in some way, but not if that disruption is caused by fear and prejudice; for example, the protection of the ADA specifically extends to people with AIDS.

There are a number of allowable exceptions to the ADA:

- Current users of illegal drugs are not protected, and alcoholics and prescription drug abusers may be held to the same standards as other workers. However, it is not permissible to discriminate against someone who has previously had a drug or alcohol abuse problem but who is no longer a user and is participating in or has completed a rehabilitation program.
- Persons who test positive for certain communicable diseases may be prevented from working in positions requiring food handling.
- If your disability would pose a direct threat to the health and safety of other workers or customers, you are not protected.

In the first full year of the law's existence almost 50 percent of the charges filed under ADA were related to employee terminations, so for disabled employees this is a powerful new vehicle for the enforcement of their rights in termination.

The Rehabilitation Act of 1973 also covers federal employees and employees of federal contractors, as well as recipients of federal assistance. Many of its provisions are similar.

If you feel that your ADA rights have been violated as the result of a termination, you should contact the EEOC. The rules are similar to those of Title VII.

Other Laws Bearing on Termination

Finally, a number of other statutes have termination-related provisions in them.

Under the Occupational Safety and Health Act (OSHA) (passed in 1970), which deals with workplace safety, you may not be fired for refusing to do unsafe work, for filing a complaint with OSHA, or for participating in the investigation of a complaint. This is one of the laws under which whistle-blowers are protected.

Under the Employee Retirement Income Security Act of 1974 (ERISA), which deals with pension plans, you may not be fired to prevent your pension benefits from vesting.

Under the Consumer Credit and Protection Act (1968), you may not be fired for a single instance of having your wages attached, such as for child support or other debts.

Under the Labor Management Relations Act (LMRA—also known as the Taft-Hartley Act, passed in 1947), you may not be fired for participating in allowable union organizing activities or for belonging to a union.

Under the Employee Polygraph Protection Act (1988), you may not be fired for refusing to take a polygraph (lie detector) test except in a few specific instances, such as if you are suspected of theft. This law does not apply to defense contractors, certain government agencies and contractors involved in national security matters, companies in security businesses (for employees involved in security work), or employees who handle prescription drugs.

Appendix I

State Termination Laws

Alabama

EEOC office address:
1900 3rd Ave. North, Ste 101
Birmingham, AL 35203
(205) 731-0082

State enforcement agency: None

Illegal discrimination: Alabama is one of the few states with no antidiscrimination legislation. The state does, however, encourage the hiring of the blind and the physically handicapped.

Blacklisting regulations: Blacklisting is prohibited and can be punished by fines or prison sentences.

Plant closing laws: None

Payment of wages after discharge: No legislation

Personnel file access: No legislation

Discharge for wage garnishment: Not permitted in the case of a child support withholding order.

Health insurance continuation: In case of plant relocation or closing, must be continued for up to 120 days.

Non-compete agreements: Allowable, but the courts have ruled that people who sign these agreements must be left with the ability to earn a living, so enforcing these agreements is difficult.

Exceptions to at-will employment doctrine: In general, the Alabama courts have been unsympathetic to finding exceptions to the at-will doctrine.

Some of the material that appears in these appendixes is from *Every Employee's Guide to the Law* by Lewin G. Joel III. Copyright © 1993 by Lewin G. Joel III. Reprinted by permission of Pantheon Books, a division of Random House, Inc.

For example, in *Harrel v. Reynolds Metals Co.* (1986), a personnel manager had offered a prospective employee a "lifetime" job, but this was held by the courts to be such an unusual guarantee that the employee should have known that a higher-level executive would have had to make the offer for it to be enforceable. Nevertheless, the Alabama courts have recognized some instances in which an *implied contract* exists and thus can be used as the basis for a wrongful discharge suit.

The Alabama legislature has defined some actions as wrongful discharges in violation of *public policy;* it disallows discharge for responding to a jury subpoena, for filing a written complaint regarding a safety violation, or for filing a workers' compensation claim. The Alabama courts, however, have steadfastly refused to expand this doctrine, saying that it is up to the state legislature to create any such regulations. This means that there is no whistle-blower protection other than that contained in the aforementioned state legislation, and the violation of public policy concept as the underpinning for a wrongful discharge suit is relatively weak.

With regard to the doctrine of *good faith and fair dealing,* Alabama does not insist that employers live up to such a standard. The Alabama Supreme Court has said specifically that it will not extend the bad faith concept into the area of general contract law.

Alaska

EEOC office address: None. Discrimination claims relating to federal law should be directed to the Seattle office (see Washington).

State enforcement agency:
Alaska Commission for Human Rights
800 "A" Street, Ste 202
Anchorage, AK 99501
(907) 274-4692

Anchorage Equal Rights Commission

Illegal discrimination: Legislation covers all employers of one or more employees. Discrimination based on the following criteria is against the law: race, religion, color, national origin (including ancestry), sex, age, physical or mental disability, marital status, changes in marital status, pregnancy, and parenthood. Discrimination claims must be filed with the state within 300 days of the claimed incident of discrimination. Penalties for breaking the law can include criminal proceedings and prison time.

Blacklisting regulations: None

Plant closing laws: None

Payment of wages after discharge: Employees who are fired or who quit must be paid their final paychecks within three days. Laid-off employees and strikers may be paid on the regular payroll schedule.

Personnel file access: Employees have access to their files, but the State Department of Labor has no authority to enforce the statute if an employer fails to comply.

Discharge for wage garnishment: Not permitted in the case of a support withholding order.

Health insurance continuation: No legislation

Non-compete agreements: No legislation

Exceptions to at-will employment doctrine: Alaska has an unusually broad set of criteria for illegal discrimination, which reduces the need for other exceptions to the at-will doctrine. In general, the state courts have been receptive to these exceptions, though Alaska is by no means the easiest state in which to win wrongful discharge suits.

The Alaska courts have recognized the concept of the *implied contract* as a basis for wrongful discharge litigation. For example, the court has ruled that an employee who was told that he had a job until retirement could be fired only for "cause." In *Bubbel v. Wien Air Alaska, Inc.* (1984), the court said that an airline's promise to pilots of permanent employment if they replaced striking pilots constituted an enforceable contract. It has also been established in Alaska that an employee handbook can modify the at-will doctrine in certain cases.

There is some indication that the Alaska courts will support the *public policy* exception to at-will employment. One statute says that employers may not retaliate against an employee for making a safety complaint. Whistle-blowers are protected if they are public employees. However, in general, the public policy concept has been joined with the *good faith and fair dealing* doctrine, which is better recognized in Alaska than in most states.

Arizona

EEOC office address:
4520 North Central Ave., Ste 300
Phoenix, AZ 85012
(602) 640-5000

State enforcement agency:
Civil Rights Division, Department of Law
Arizona Attorney General's Office
1275 West Washington St., Room 102
Phoenix, AZ 85007
(602) 542-5263

402 West Congress, Ste 314
Tucson, AZ 85701
(602) 628-6500

Illegal discrimination: Legislation covers all employers of fifteen or more employees. Discrimination based on the following criteria is against the law: race, color, religion, sex, age, AIDS, handicap, national origin. High-level executives with pensions of $27,000 per year or more may be forced to retire at age 65. Public employees must retire at age 70. Discrimination claims must be filed with the state within 180 days of the claimed incident of discrimination.

Blacklisting legislation: Blacklisting is prohibited.

Plant closing laws: None

Payment of wages after discharge: Fired employees must be paid within three working days or on the next regularly scheduled payday, whichever is sooner. Employees who quit must be paid by the next regular payday.

Personnel file access: Available to public employees only.

Discharge for wage garnishment: Prohibited

Health insurance continuation: No legislation

Non-compete agreements: No legislation

Exceptions to at-will employment doctrine: In general, the Arizona courts have been open-minded in allowing exceptions to the at-will employment doctrine.

With regard to the *implied contract* concept, the court has recognized the idea that employee handbooks and other expressions of employer policies can be used as the basis for a suit alleging that an employment contract has been breached.

Whistle-blowers are protected in Arizona if they are public employees, and in general the *public policy* exception to at-will employment is very strong. Employees cannot be fired for filing workers' compensation claims, and employer retaliation is outlawed when an employee files a safety complaint. The courts have not insisted that a specific law be violated for the public policy doctrine to be invoked, but merely that a more general "public policy interest" be violated.

The concept of *good faith and fair dealing* has been slightly accepted by the courts. It would be unusual for the Arizona courts to void a discharge under this doctrine, but the concept of fair treatment has been upheld.

Arkansas

EEOC office address:
425 West Capitol Ave., 6th Floor
Little Rock, AR 72201
(501) 324-5060

State enforcement agency: Employees of private employers should go directly to the EEOC. Most Arkansas state employees can go first to their agency's grievance office, though they may go directly to the EEOC if they wish. The location of a particular agency's grievance office can be found by calling the State Employee Grievance Appeal Panel at (501) 682-1507.

Illegal discrimination: As of 1993, Arkansas has an antidiscrimination statute. Legislation covers all employers of nine or more employees. Discrimination based on the following criteria is against the law: race; religion; ancestry; national origin; gender (including pregnancy); or sensory, mental, or physical disability. Discrimination claims must be filed within 365 days of the claimed incident of discrimination. Unlike some state laws, Arkansas provides for compensatory and punitive damages.

Blacklisting regulations: Prohibited, and punishable by fines or prison sentences.

Plant closing laws: None

Payment of wages after discharge: Fired employees must be paid within seven days. Employees who quit must be paid by the next regular payday.

Personnel file access: Available only to public employees, under the state Freedom of Information Act. Employees of nongovernmental organizations are guaranteed no access to their files.

Discharge for wage garnishment: A noncustodial parent may not be fired for a child support garnishment.

Health insurance continuation: No legislation

Non-compete agreements: No legislation

Exceptions to at-will employment doctrine: In general, Arkansas is a backward state when it comes to the at-will employment doctrine, and it is difficult to get the state courts to go along with exceptions.

There has been some minor willingness to accept the *implied contract* doctrine in cases where employee handbooks strongly suggest a long-term employment relationship. The *public policy* exception has been allowed in cases of terminations for filing workers' compensation claims, and employees may not be discharged for filing a wage claim or for serving on a jury. There is no whistle-blower protection. The Arkansas courts have not recognized the concept of *good faith and fair dealing* as a basis for deviating from employment at will.

California

EEOC office addresses:

1265 West Shaw Ave., Ste 103
Fresno, CA 93711
(209) 487-5793

401 B St., Ste 1550
San Diego, CA 92101
(619) 557-7235

255 East Temple St., 4th Floor
Los Angeles, CA 90012
(213) 894-1000

901 Market St., Ste 500
San Francisco, CA 94103
(415) 744-6500

1301 Clay St., Ste 1170-N
Oakland, CA 94612
(510) 637-3230

96 North 3rd St.
San Jose, CA 95112
(408) 291-7352

State enforcement agency:
California Dept. of Fair Employment and Housing
2014 T St., Ste 210
Sacramento, CA 95814
(916) 445-9918

Illegal discrimination: Legislation covers all employers of five or more employees. Discrimination based on the following criteria is against the law: race, religion, color, national origin, ancestry, physical or mental disability (specifically including AIDS), pregnancy, medical condition, marital status, sex, age, actual or perceived sexual orientation, usually non-conviction arrests. Antidiscrimination rules for mental disability apply to employers of fifteen or more employees.

Discrimination claims must be filed with the state within one year of the claimed incident of discrimination. High-level executives with pensions of $27,000 per year or higher may be forced to retire at age 65.

Blacklisting regulations: Prohibited, and punishable by fines and prison sentences.

Plant closing laws: None

Payment of wages after discharge: Fired employees must be paid immediately. Employees who quit must be paid within three days. Strikers must be paid by the next regular payday.

Personnel file access: All employees have access to their personnel files, not including written reference letters.

Discharge for wage garnishment: Not permitted for a single judgment.

Health insurance continuation: No legislation

Non-compete agreements: Prohibited except in specific circumstances. It is difficult to enforce these agreements unless the departing employee had been a meaningful owner or partner of the employer.

Exceptions to at-will employment doctrine: California historically has been one of the most liberal states in finding exceptions to the concept of at-will employment, but indications are that this may be tightening.

The *implied contract* concept has been upheld in a variety of circumstances. In *Collins v. Shell Oil Co.* (1991), an executive was awarded $5.3 million for breach of a lifetime contract, punitive damages, and noneconomic losses in a case where the employee had been told that satisfactory work would result in being part of the "family" for life. This was also a case in which issues of the employee's sexual orientation and the employer's falsification of performance evaluations were involved.

In another case, even an employee handbook statement to the effect that all employees were at-will employees was deemed insufficient; the court ruled that in fact it was the employer's practice to fire people only for good cause, so good cause was required in the specific case. There have been at least two cases where long-term employment in and of itself was regarded as having compromised the at-will doctrine and made discharge more difficult.

The *public policy* exception also is well established; in fact, California, in *Petermann v. Teamsters* (1959), was the first state to introduce this doctrine. Employees are protected from discharge for refusing to violate a safety code, for serving on a jury, for filing a workers' compensation claim, for testifying as a witness in an official proceeding, for disclosing their wages, and for many other reasons. Whistle-blowers, including private sector employees, are protected.

California courts have also been among the most liberal in requiring *good faith and fair dealing* on the part of employers. For example, wrongful discharge suits have been allowed in situations where the employer typically has fired people only for good cause and thus created a presumption that this would be the standard used in all terminations. In the now famous *Foley* case (765 P.2d 373) in 1988, the "good faith and fair dealing" concept was explicitly upheld, but this same suit also reaffirmed that employees in the state are subject to the at-will doctrine; on balance, *Foley* made it harder for a fired employee to win a wrongful discharge suit.

Colorado

EEOC office address:
303 East 17th St., Ste 510
Denver, CO 80203
(303) 866-1300

State Enforcement Agency:
Colorado Civil Rights Commission
1560 Broadway, Ste 1050
Denver, CO 80202
(303) 894-2997

For Colorado state employees:
Colorado State Personnel Board
1313 Sherman St., Room 111
Denver, CO 80203
(303) 866-3244

Illegal discrimination: Legislation covers all employers with one or more employees. Discrimination based on the following criteria is against the law: handicap (specifically including AIDS), race, creed, color, sex, age, national origin, ancestry, and marriage to a co-worker. Discrimination claims must be filed within six months of the claimed incident of discrimination.

Blacklisting regulations: Prohibited, and punishable by fines or prison sentences.

Plant closing laws: None

Payment of wages after discharge: Fired employees must be paid immediately. Employees who quit and strikers may be paid on the next regular payday.

Personnel file access: No legislation, but if written reference information is provided by a past employer to a prospective employer, a copy must be sent to your last known address by your past employer.

Discharge for wage garnishment: Not allowable if the garnishment is for support or a consumer credit transaction.

Health insurance continuation: No legislation

Non-compete agreements: Prohibited except for the protection of trade secrets, for the recovery of training expenses from those employed for less than two years, and for executive- and management-level personnel and professional staff.

Exceptions to at-will employment doctrine: Colorado is about in the middle among the states with regard to its willingness to void the at-will employment concept.

Colorado courts generally have held that the employee handbook creates an *implied contract* between employer and employee. Thus, in cases where such a handbook implies a permanent employment relationship, the employer will be so bound by the courts. However, the Colorado courts have thus far refused to accept oral statements as having created such a contract, whereas in some states an oral promise is sufficient.

Colorado only recently accepted the *public policy* exception to employment at will. However, the courts acknowledged this concept in 1988 in a case in which a discharge was voided on behalf of an an employee who had refused to violate a state law and then testified about his and his employer's actions. The Colorado Supreme Court has laid down very specific guidelines for wrongful discharge cases relating to an employee's refusal to perform an illegal act. A whistle-blower statute protects state employees, but private employees are covered only by individual court cases, not by legislation. In addition, employees cannot be discharged for serving on a jury or participating in legitimate union activities.

The Colorado courts have never as yet supported the requirement for *good faith and fair dealing* by employers, and thus it has not been used successfully in wrongful discharge cases.

Connecticut

EEOC office address: None. Discrimination claims under federal law should be filed with the Boston office (see Massachusetts).

State enforcement agency:
Connecticut Commission on Human Rights and Opportunities
90 Washington St.
Hartford, CT 06106
(203) 566-3350

Also the New Haven Commission on Equal Opportunities

Illegal discrimination: Legislation covers all employers of three or more employees. Discrimination based on the following criteria is against the law: race, color, religious creed, age (all ages rather than the 40-plus criterion used in federal law), sex (including pregnancy), sexual orientation, marital status, national origin, ancestry, present or past history of mental disorder, mental retardation, learning disability, physical disability, and criminal conviction record (for state employees only). Discrimination claims must be filed within 180 days of the claimed incident of discrimination. Executives with pension entitlements equal to or greater than $44,000 per year may be forced to retire at age 65.

Blacklisting regulations: Prohibited, and punishable by fines.

Plant closing laws: See Health insurance continuation section below.

Payment of wages after discharge: Fired employees must be paid on the next work day. Employees who quit or are laid off, and strikers, may be paid on the next regular payday.

Personnel file access: Employees have access to their files but not to written reference letters.

Discharge for wage garnishment: Allowed only for more than seven garnishments in one year.

Health insurance continuation: Terminated employees can continue in the health insurance plan for up to thirty-nine weeks after termination by paying the group insurance rate. If an employee is terminated because the business closes or relocates, and the employer had 100 or more employees for a year or longer, the employer must continue the health insurance plan for 120 days.

Non-compete agreements: No legislation

Exceptions to at-will employment doctrine: Although not as open-minded as California, Connecticut is one of the states more willing to allow exceptions to employment at will, and thus a state where wrongful discharge suits are easiest to win.

There have been a limited number of cases testing the *implied contract* concept, but the state courts have upheld the idea.

Public policy violation as a basis for wrongful discharge litigation has been broadly applied. There are statutes that make it illegal to discharge someone for serving on a jury, for reporting a violation of law (whistle-blower protection), for filing a workers' compensation claim, or for participating in legitimate union activities. The courts also have held that firing someone to avoid paying a bonus violated the wage legislation in the state (*Cook v. Alexander and Alexander of Connecticut*, 1985).

With regard to *good faith and fair dealing,* the Connecticut court rulings have been a bit confusing. The concept that an employer must deal fairly with employees has been established, but the idea that good cause is required for a discharge to take place is not well established. As a result, fired employees are on safer grounds in wrongful discharge suits if a public policy violation can be established.

Delaware

EEOC office address: None. Discrimination claims relating to federal law should be filed with the Philadelphia office (see Pennsylvania).

State enforcement agency:
Delaware Department of Labor
Anti-Discrimination Section
State Office Bldg., 6th Floor
820 North French St.
Wilmington, DE 19801
(302) 577-2900

Illegal discrimination: Legislation covers all employers of four or more employees. Discrimination based on the following criteria is against the law: race, marital status, color, age, religion, sex, national origin. Discrimination against the handicapped is also forbidden for employers of twenty or more employees. High-level executives may be required to retire at age 65 if their pension rights are greater than or equal to $27,000 per year. Discrimination claims must be filed with the state within ninety days of the claimed incident of discrimination or within 120 days of the discovery of the incident, whichever is later.

Blacklisting regulations: None

Plant closing laws: None

Payment of wages after discharge: All terminated employees must be paid by the next regular payday.

Personnel file access: Employees have access to their files other than to reference letters.

Discharge for wage garnishment: Not allowed

Health insurance continuation: No legislation

Non-compete agreements: Prohibited for physicians only.

Exceptions to at-will employment doctrine: For the most part, Delaware is living in the Dark Ages as regards wrongful discharge suits. This may be part of the attractiveness of the state as the legal headquarters of many corporations that are actually located elsewhere. Delaware is one of only a handful of states that essentially allow no exceptions to the employment at will concept.

The *implied contract* argument has specifically been rejected by the Delaware courts, and the employee handbook cannot be used as the basis of a breach of contract suit. Only a few states have taken such a strongly negative position.

Certain statutes allow for *public policy* litigation, but these are standard laws prohibiting discharge for serving on a jury or filing a wage claim. The broader public policy concept is not well established; that is, it is difficult to win a wrongful discharge suit unless there is a specific law prohibiting discharge under specific circumstances. However, whistle-blowers are reasonably well protected if they are state or public school employees.

There is no requirement that Delaware employers treat their employees with *good faith and fair dealing*.

District of Columbia

EEOC office address:
1400 L St., NW, Ste 200
Washington, DC 20005
(202) 275-7377

The national headquarters of the EEOC is located at:

1801 L St., NW
Washington, DC 20507
(202) 663-4264

District enforcement agency:
Human Rights Commission
441 4th St., NW
Washington, DC 20001
(202) 724-1385

Illegal discrimination: Legislation covers all employers of one or more employees. Discrimination based on the following criteria is against the law: race, color, religion, national origin, sex, ages 18 to 65, marital status, personal appearance (such as hair style and beards, but not including cleanliness or body type), sexual orientation, family responsibilities, physical handicap (specifically including AIDS), matriculation, and political affiliation. Discrimination claims must be filed with the District within one year of the claimed incident of discrimination.

Blacklisting regulations: None

Plant closing laws: None

Payment of wages after discharge: Fired employees must be paid on the next workday, except for employees responsible for handling money, who may be paid as late as four working days after firing. Employees who quit must be paid within one week or by the next regular payday, whichever is sooner. Strikers must be paid by the next regular payday.

Personnel file access: Only employees of the District of Columbia have access to their files.

Discharge for wage garnishment: Not allowed

Health insurance continuation: No legislation

Non-compete agreements: No legislation

Exceptions to at-will employment doctrine: The District of Columbia is a bit more liberal than average in recognizing exceptions to at-will employment. The District courts probably would be more liberal but for the fact that District statutes offer so many avenues for illegal discrimination lawsuits that exceptions to the at-will doctrine are less necessary than in some states.

Employees have been allowed to pursue the *implied contract* doctrine on the basis of statements in employee handbooks. However, there is some indication in the case law that the employee must have been aware of the content of the handbook and thus have known that a binding contract had been created. In *Hodge v. Evans Financial* (1987), the court also allowed a wrongful discharge claim based on an oral promise of permanent employment.

The *public policy* exception has been defined very narrowly here. Specifically, the courts have held that an employee may sue for wrongful discharge only if the employee's refusal to violate the law was the sole reason for the discharge, and the burden of proof for this claim is on the employee. There is no specific legislation protecting whistle-blowers except that public employees get some protection. There is also a statute outlawing discharge for making a wage claim.

As a stand-alone basis for an exception, the *good faith and fair dealing* concept is not well established in the District court.

Florida

EEOC office addresses:

1 NE 1st St., 6th Floor
Miami, FL 33132
(305) 536-4491

501 East Polk St., 10th Floor
Tampa, FL 33602
(813) 228-2310

State enforcement agency:
Florida Commission on Human Relations
325 John Knox Rd.
Building F, Ste 240
Tallahassee, FL 32303
(904) 488-7082

The following also are 706 agencies:

Broward County Human Relations Commission
Clearwater Office of Community Relations
St. Petersburg Human Relations Department
Jacksonville Equal Employment Opportunity Commission
Dade County Fair Housing and Employment Commission
Hillsborough County Equal Employment and Human Relations
     Department
Lee County Department of Equal Opportunity
Orlando Human Relations Department
Tampa Office of Community Relations

Illegal discrimination: Legislation covers all employers of fifteen or more employees. Discrimination based on the following criteria is against the law: race, color, sex, religion, AIDS, age (all ages), handicap, marital status, pregnancy, sickle-cell disease, and political activity. Discrimination claims must be filed within 365 days of the claimed incident of discrimination.

Blacklisting regulations: Prohibited, and punishable by fines.

Plant closing laws: None

Payment of wages after discharge: No legislation

Personnel file access: Available only for the purpose of examining medical records that may indicate exposure to toxic substances.

Discharge for wage garnishment: Not allowed if based on garnishment for support payments.

Health insurance continuation: No legislation

Non-compete agreements: Allowed

Exceptions to at-will employment doctrine: Florida, like many southern states, is behind the rest of the country in recognizing exceptions to the at-will doctrine, and it is very difficult in this state to win a wrongful discharge suit.

Florida courts recognize nothing short of a written employment contract specifying a definite period of time. They do not recognize the concept that an employee handbook or oral statement can create an *implied contract.*

The only specific situation in which Florida has allowed a wrongful discharge suit for violation of *public policy* involved an employee's right to file for workers' compensation benefits. The state also has a law protecting employees from discharge for serving on a jury. Whistle-blowers are protected if they are public employees.

Florida courts have not recognized the *good faith and fair dealing* exception to at-will employment.

Georgia

EEOC office addresses:
75 Piedmont Ave., NE,
Ste 1100
Atlanta, GA 30335
(404) 331-6408

410 Mall Blvd., Ste G
Savannah, GA 31406
(912) 652-4234

State enforcement agency:
Georgia Commission on Equal Opportunity
Equal Employment Division
17 Cain Tower
229 Peachtree St., N.E.
Atlanta, GA 30303
(404) 656-1736

Richmond County Human Rights Commission

Illegal discrimination: Georgia does not have the typical all-purpose antidiscrimination legislation covering private employers. A specific age discrimination law roughly conforms to federal law, and employers of fifteen or more employees cannot discriminate on the basis of handicaps. Public employees are protected by the standard discrimination criteria: race, color, religion, national origin, sex, physical handicap, and age.

Blacklisting regulations: None

Plant closing laws: None

Payment of wages after discharge: No legislation

Personnel file access: No legislation

Discharge for wage garnishment: Prohibited for garnishments based on a single indebtedness.

Health insurance continuation: Available for three months unless the employee has been terminated for cause, or the health insurance contract has been terminated for the entire organization, or the necessary contributions have not been paid by the employee.

Non-compete agreements: No legislation. Georgia courts have ruled that customer lists are not trade secrets and thus cannot form the basis for a non-compete agreement. They also have ruled that a non-compete agreement cannot extend geographically to states in which the employee has not worked for that employer.

Exceptions to at-will employment doctrine: Georgia is one of the most pro-employer, anti-employee states in the union. It is virtually a waste of time to bring wrongful discharge suits to the Georgia courts. Even in the South it is the most conservative of states.

Specifically, there have been no cases supporting employee handbook wording as the basis for an *implied contract,* and only very specific employment contracts, with precise employment periods spelled out, have been upheld. For example, such phrases as "permanent employment" and "employment for life" are not considered sufficient to create a contract. Neither have oral statements been allowed to create implied contracts.

Georgia law requires that employees be given time off to vote, but the courts do not support the use of *public policy* violations as the basis for wrongful discharge suits. There is no whistle-blower protection. The courts also do not require Georgia employers to practice *good faith and fair dealing* when interacting with employees.

Hawaii

EEOC office address:
677 Ala Moana Blvd., Ste 404
Honolulu, HI 96813
(808) 541-3120

State enforcement agency:
Hawaii Department of Labor and Industrial Relations
Civil Rights Commission
888 Mililani St., 2nd Floor
Honolulu, HI 96813
(808) 586-8636

Illegal discrimination: Legislation covers all employers of one or more employees. Discrimination based on the following criteria is against the law: race, sex (including pregnancy), sexual orientation, age, color, religion, ancestry, national origin, disabilities, marital status, and arrest or court record unless it has substantial relationship to the job functions.

Blacklisting regulations: Prohibited.

Plant closing laws: Employers of fifty or more employees who downsize, relocate, or close their facility must give forty-five days' written notice and must pay a dislocated worker an allowance equal to four weeks of the difference (if any) between the average weekly wage and the rate of unemployment compensation.

Payment of wages after discharge: Fired employees must be paid immediately. Employees who quit, strikers, and laid-off employees must be paid by the next regular payday, although employees who quit must be paid immediately if they have given two weeks' notice.

Personnel file access: Available only for government employees, under the state Freedom of Information Act.

Discharge for wage garnishment: Not permitted if the garnishment is for child support.

Health insurance continuation: No legislation

Non-compete agreements: Allowable with regard to trade secrets.

Exceptions to at-will employment doctrine: Hawaii is about average among the states in its willingness to consider at-will exceptions.

In general, the Hawaiian courts have not encouraged litigation based on the *implied contract* doctrine. There has been some limited recognition of the binding nature of an employee handbook, but the handbook must be quite specific to be usable in a wrongful discharge suit.

The *public policy* concept is quite well established. Hawaii has a variety of laws protecting employees from discharge for refusing to operate dangerous equipment or for engaging in union activity. Employers are also prohibited from retaliating against employees who file safety complaints or wage claims and who report a violation of law to a government entity. Whistle-blowers are protected. The courts have stated that public policy may be contained in both the letter and the purpose of the law.

The courts have refused to try to interpret the meaning of *good faith and fair dealing,* so this is not a productive avenue for wrongful discharge suits in Hawaii.

Idaho

EEOC office address: None. Discrimination claims under federal law should be filed with the EEOC office in Seattle (see Washington).

State enforcement agency:
Idaho Commission on Human Rights
450 West State St.
Boise, ID 83720
(208) 334-2873

Illegal discrimination: Legislation covers all employers of five or more employees. Discrimination based on the following criteria is against the law: race, color, religion, sex, national origin, age, handicap, and pregnancy. Discrimination claims must be filed within one year of the claimed incident of discrimination.

Blacklisting regulations: None

Plant closing laws: None

Payment of wages after discharge: All terminated employees must be paid within ten working days or on the next regular payday, whichever is sooner.

Personnel file access: Available only to government employees under the state Freedom of Information Act.

Discharge for wage garnishment: Not allowed for garnishments related to support payments or consumer credit transactions.

Health insurance continuation: No legislation

Non-compete agreements: No legislation

Exceptions to at-will employment doctrine: Somewhat surprisingly, given its lack of big cities and the rural nature of the state, Idaho is among the more progressive states in allowing exceptions to the at-will doctrine.

The courts have ruled that both employee handbooks and statements by supervisory and management personnel can be used as the basis for creating an *implied contract.*

The state also recognizes *public policy* exceptions to the at-will rule. Employees may not be discharged for union activity or retaliated against for filing a wage claim. The courts also have said more broadly that a discharge may be wrongful if contrary to public policy, but there is no specific whistle-blower protection.

As of 1989, Idaho has also recognized the concept of *good faith and fair dealing.* However, the Idaho Supreme Court has said that this does not mean that employers may terminate employees only for "good cause." This means that any such lawsuits will be complex ones.

Illinois

EEOC office address:
500 West Madison St., 28th Floor
Chicago, IL 60661
(312) 353-2713

State enforcement agency:
Illinois Department of Human Rights
100 West Randolph St., Ste 10–100
Chicago, IL 60601
(312) 814-6200

Bloomington Human Relations Commission

Illegal discrimination: Legislation covers all employers of fifteen or more employees. Discrimination based on the following criteria is against the law: race, color, religion, national origin, ancestry, age, sex, marital status, physical or mental handicap, unfavorable discharge from military service, arrest or conviction record. Discrimination claims must be filed within 180 days of the claimed incident of discrimination.

Blacklisting regulations: Prohibited, and punishable with fines or prison sentences.

Plant closing laws: None

Payment of wages after discharge: Fired employees and employees who quit must be paid immediately if possible, but no later than the next regular payday. Strikers and laid-off employees must be paid by the next regular payday.

Personnel file access: Employers of five or more employees must permit employees to review their files, not including letters of reference, test documents, and records of court proceedings or criminal investigations.

Discharge for wage garnishment: Not allowed for garnishments associated with a single indebtedness.

Health insurance continuation: If the group policy permits, terminated employees may keep group coverage for six months if they have been covered for three months prior to termination. This election must be made within ten days of termination.

Non-compete agreements: No legislation

Exceptions to at-will employment doctrine: Illinois, like other very large urban states, has a long history of wrongful discharge litigation. Overall, the Illinois courts have been a bit more progressive than average in finding exceptions to the at-will doctrine, and have been especially liberal with regard to public policy violations.

In general, the courts in Illinois feel that employee handbooks do not create *implied contracts*. However, a handbook can become such a contract if three criteria are met: (1) It contains a clear promise that an employee could reasonably interpret as an offer; (2) the handbook has been given to the employee so that there is employee awareness of the offer; and (3) the employee accepts the offer by starting or continuing to work. On the other hand, disclaimers in the handbook (that is, statements that employees are covered by the at-will doctrine) generally have been upheld by the courts.

Illinois employees may file for wrongful discharge if a *public policy* violation has occurred. Whistle-blowers are protected if they are state employees, as are employees who file workers' compensation claims. Employees have also been protected for refusing to handle radioactive materials unsafely and for refusing to violate the Internal Revenue Code and Securities and Exchange Commission regulations. In fact, Illinois is one of the states that has interpreted the public policy violation concept most broadly.

Illinois does not require *good faith and fair dealing* by its employers.

Indiana

EEOC office address:
101 West Ohio St., Ste 1900
Indianapolis, IN 46204
(317) 226-7212

State enforcement agency:
Indiana Civil Rights Commission
100 North Senate Ave., Room N-103
Indianapolis, IN 46204
(317) 232-2600

Anderson Human Relations Commission
Bloomington Human Rights Commission
East Chicago Human Relations Commission
Evansville Human Relations Commission
Fort Wayne Metropolitan Human Relations Commission
Gary Human Relations Commission
Michigan City Human Rights Commission
South Bend Human Rights Commission

Illegal discrimination: Legislation covers all employers of six or more employees. Discrimination based on the following criteria is against the law: race, religion, color, sex, disability (covers employers with fifteen or more employees), national origin, ancestry, ages 40 to 70. Discrimination claims must be filed within 180 days of the claimed incident of discrimination.

Blacklisting regulations: Prohibited for railroad employees only.

Plant closing laws: None

Payment of wages after discharge: All terminated employees must be paid by the next regular payday.

Personnel file access: Files are available to government employees only.

Discharge for wage garnishment: Discharge is not allowed for any type of garnishment.

Health insurance continuation: No legislation

Non-compete agreements: No legislation

Exceptions to at-will employment doctrine: Indiana is a relatively difficult state in which to win a wrongful discharge suit, but there have been some exceptions.

In general, the Indiana courts have not recognized the use of employee handbooks as creating an *implied contract*. However, if an employee does something to his or her own detriment because of a belief that permanent employment has been guaranteed, the courts may support the idea that an implied contract exists. Examples might be waiving one's rights to sue for a job-related injury or abandoning a competing business to accept employment. Notwithstanding this exception, it is difficult to win a wrongful discharge case in Indiana on implied contract grounds.

Public policy exceptions to the at-will doctrine exist. A court decision has laid down that employees may not be fired for filing workers' compensation claims (Indiana was the first state to have such a ruling, in 1973), and certain statutes make it illegal to retaliate against employees for making a safety complaint or wage claim or for reporting violations of the law. Whistle-blowers are protected if they work for the state or for government contractors, if they care for the elderly, and in certain other narrow circumstances. The actual court experience in this state, however, is that wrongful discharge suits related to workers' compensation are the ones most likely to succeed.

The Indiana courts have not recognized the rule of *good faith and fair dealing.*

Iowa

EEOC office address: None. Discrimination claims under federal law should be filed with the EEOC office in Milwaukee (see Wisconsin).

State enforcement agency:
Iowa Civil Rights Commission
211 East Maple St., 2nd Floor
Grimes State Office Bldg.
Des Moines, IA 50319
(515) 281-4121

Fort Dodge-Webster County Human Rights Commission
Mason City Human Rights Commission

Illegal discrimination: Legislation covers all employers except those who regularly employ only one to three employees. Discrimination based on the following criteria is against the law: age (18 or older), race, color, creed, sex, national origin, religion, pregnancy, and non–job-related physical or mental handicap (specifically including AIDS). Discrimination claims must be filed within 180 days of the claimed incident of discrimination.

Blacklisting regulations: Prohibited, and punishable by fines and damages.

Plant closing laws: None.

Payment of wages after discharge: Both fired employees and employees who quit must be paid by the next regular payday.

Personnel file access: Employees have access to their personnel files but not to letters of reference.

Discharge for wage garnishment: Prohibited

Health insurance continuation: In the case of a layoff, employees may continue coverage for up to six months by paying group rates if they have previously been members of the plan for six months.

Non-compete agreements: No legislation

Exceptions to at-will employment doctrine: Iowa courts have created exceptions to the at-will employment concept, but only in narrow circumstances. In general, the state tends to be very employer-friendly.

In certain situations, Iowa has permitted employee handbooks to be construed as creating an *implied contract.* However, the handbook must be quite precise in stating that termination will occur only for just cause or in other specific circumstances, and it must be clear that the employee received the handbook and understood the contractual nature of the relationship. In a variety of cases, handbooks have not been accepted by the courts as creating a contract in spite of loosely worded statements in the handbook that suggested otherwise.

There is state legislation that makes it unlawful to fire an employee for complaining about exposure to hazardous materials or for filing a safety complaint. Nevertheless, the *public policy* doctrine is more weakly established in Iowa than in most other states. The courts have accepted the concept that certain whistle-blowers are to be protected and that the public policy doctrine exists, but it is difficult for a plaintiff (a fired employee filing a lawsuit) to get the Iowa courts to apply this principle to real situations.

Iowa does not recognize the concept of *good faith and fair dealing* in wrongful discharge suits.

Kansas

EEOC office address: None. Discrimination claims under federal law should be filed at the EEOC office in St. Louis (see Missouri).

State enforcement agency:
Kansas Human Rights Commission
Landon State Office Building
900 Southwest Jackson, Suite 851 South
Topeka, KS 66612
(913) 296-3206

Salina Human Relation Commission and Department
Topeka Human Relations Commission

Illegal discrimination: Legislation covers all employers of four or more employees. Discrimination based on the following criteria is against the law: race, religion, color, age (18 or older), sex, physical disability, national origin, and ancestry. Executives may be forced to retire at age 65 if their pension entitlement is equal to or greater than $44,000 per year. Discrimination claims must be filed within six months of the claimed incident of discrimination.

Blacklisting regulations: Prohibited, and punishable by fines or prison sentences.

Plant closing laws: Legislation covers only selected industries and relatively narrow circumstances.

Payment of wages after discharge: All terminated employees must be paid by the next regular payday.

Personnel file access: No legislation

Discharge for wage garnishment: Prohibited

Health insurance continuation: Terminated employees can continue coverage for up to six months at the group rate if they have been covered by the plan for at least three months prior to termination.

Non-compete agreements: No legislation

Exceptions to at-will employment doctrine: Kansas is relatively liberal in providing exceptions to the employment at will doctrine, and in some cases has allowed broad interpretations of the conditions under which exceptions will be granted.

The state courts have shown a willingness to recognize the *implied contract* exception on the basis of statements in employee handbooks and on that of oral statements as well. In *Johnson v. National Beef Packing Co.* (1976), the court said that it would take into account such factors as longevity of employment, the nature of that employment, employee handbooks, performance evaluations, oral promises, and the giving up of other job opportunities. This is one of the broader statements of the implied contract doctrine found in the state laws.

Like many states, Kansas forbids termination for testifying in certain government proceedings and for filing a wage or workers' compensation claim. The courts also have said more generally that violations of *public policy* are grounds for wrongful discharge suits, and have specifically protected whistle-blowers if they are public employees.

The Kansas courts have not accepted the concept of *good faith and fair dealing*.

Kentucky

EEOC office address:
600 Martin Luther King Jr. Place, Ste 268
Louisville, KY 40202
(502) 582-6082

State enforcement agency:
Kentucky Commission on Human Rights
832 Capital Plaza Tower
500 Mero Street
Frankfort, KY 40601
(502) 564-3550

Paducah Human Rights Commission
Lexington-Lafayette Urban County Human Rights Commission
Louisville and Jefferson City Human Relations Commission

Illegal discrimination: Legislation covers all employers of eight or more employees. Discrimination based on the following criteria is against the law: race, color, religion, national origin, sex, age, and physical handicap (specifically including AIDS). Discrimination claims must be filed within 180 days of the claimed incident of discrimination.

Blacklisting regulations: None

Plant closing laws: None

Payment of wages after discharge: All terminated employees must be paid by the next regular pay period or within fourteen days, whichever is later.

Personnel file access: Available only to public employees.

Discharge for wage garnishment: Prohibited for a single indebtedness.

Health insurance continuation: Fired employees can continue coverage for up to nine months if they have been covered for at least three months before termination.

Non-compete agreements: No legislation

Exceptions to at-will employment doctrine: The Kentucky courts have allowed some exceptions to the at-will employment doctrine, but in general the state is about average as a place for wrongful discharge suits.

Wrongful discharge suits have successfully been brought for violation of *implied contracts* on the basis of both employee handbooks and oral statements. In *Shah v. American Synthetic Rubber Corp.* (1983), an employee who had left one position and abandoned certain employee benefits with a promise that at the new job he would be fired only for cause after a ninety-day probation period had passed was successful in bringing a wrongful discharge suit when fired.

Kentucky legislation protects employees from discharge for attending a required official proceeding, and retaliation is outlawed for filing a safety or wage complaint. The courts have also recognized that filing workers' compensation claims and engaging in legitimate union activity is protected. Whistle-blowers are protected if they are public employees, and in general the *public policy* argument has had some success.

Good faith and fair dealing is not recognized in Kentucky.

Louisiana

EEOC office address:
701 Loyola Ave., Ste 600
New Orleans, LA 70113
(504) 589-2329

State enforcement agency:
Louisiana Commission on Human Rights
1001 North 23rd Street, Box 94094
Baton Rouge, LA 70804
(504) 342-3075

Illegal discrimination: Legislation covers all employers of fifteen or more employees. Discrimination based on the following criteria is against the law: race, creed, color, religion, sex, national origin, pregnancy, physical and mental handicap other than chronic alcoholism and drug addiction. Discrimination claims must be filed within 180 days of the claimed incident of discrimination.

Blacklisting regulations: None

Plant closing laws: None

Payment of wages after discharge: Fired employees and employees who quit must be paid within three days.

Personnel file access: Available to public employees only.

Discharge for wage garnishment: Not allowed for support garnishment or for any single indebtedness. Discharge is allowed if there are garnishments for three or more unrelated debts in a two-year period.

Health insurance continuation: No legislation

Non-compete agreements: Allowed if the geographic boundaries are specified and the term is less than two years.

Exceptions to at-will employment doctrine: Although state courts have permitted some exceptions to at-will employment, in general Louisiana is regarded as a state where wrongful discharge suits are hard to win and where the courts have not finally settled on a single point of view with regard to each type of exception.

For example, the courts have accepted the idea that it is possible to amend the at-will employment relationship with an oral *implied contract*. However, the grounds in the specific cases in which this has been done are quite narrow and it is difficult to generalize from them.

Louisiana laws make it illegal to fire someone for serving on a jury, for filing a workers' compensation claim, or for reporting environmental violations. In general, the courts seem sympathetic to *public policy* violations as the basis for a wrongful discharge suit. Whistle-blowers are protected.

Very little has been said in Louisiana about *good faith and fair dealing* as the basis for litigation. As in most states, this is the least likely avenue of success.

Maine

EEOC office address: None. Discrimination complaints under federal law should be filed with the EEOC office in Boston (see Massachusetts).

State enforcement agency:
Maine Human Rights Commission
State House, Station 51
Augusta, ME 04333
(207) 624-6050

Illegal discrimination: Legislation covers all employers of one or more employees. Discrimination based on the following criteria is against the law: race, color, sex, physical or mental disability, religion, age (all ages), ancestry, national origin, and pregnancy. Discrimination claims must be filed within six months of the claimed incident of discrimination.

Blacklisting regulations: Prohibited, and punishable with fines or prison sentences.

Plant closing laws: In cases where 100 or more employees are involved and a plant is closing or relocating outside the state of Maine, employees must be given sixty days of notice and one week of severance pay for each year of service if the employee has worked at that facility for three years or longer. This severance payment is not required if the employer has a pension plan covering all employees.

Payment of wages after discharge: Employees who are fired or who quit must be paid on the next regular payday or within two weeks, whichever is sooner.

Personnel file access: Employees have access to their personnel files.

Discharge for wage garnishment: Prohibited

Health insurance continuation: Employees who have been members of the health insurance plan for at least six months are entitled to continue in the plan after termination for six months (if partially incapacitated from a work-related illness) or for twelve months (if fully incapacitated).

Non-compete agreements: No legislation

Exceptions to at-will employment doctrine: Maine historically has been reluctant to allow exceptions to at-will employment, and must be regarded as a state in which wrongful discharge cases are difficult to win.

The *implied contract* concept has been recognized in Maine in that the courts have acknowledged that such a contract may exist because of statements in the employee handbook or because of oral statements by the employer that an employee would be fired only for good cause. However, there have been few cases in Maine in which an ex-employee successfully sued for breach of this implied contract in spite of the court's philosophical acceptance of the idea.

Maine has laws that prohibit firing an employee for filing a workers' compensation claim or wage claim or for reporting a violation of law. Whistle-blowers are protected. The courts have also recognized in principle that *public policy* may be used in a wrongful discharge suit, but as yet have not allowed any such suits to go forward. As with the implied contract example, the Maine courts seem inclined to accept a philosophical premise but then to do nothing about it.

There has been no recognition of the concept of *good faith and fair dealing.*

Maryland

EEOC office address:
10 South Howard St., 3rd Floor
Baltimore, MD 21201
(410) 962-3932

State enforcement agency:
Maryland Commission on Human Relations
20 East Franklin St.
Baltimore, MD 21202
(410) 333-1700

Baltimore Community Relations Commission
Howard County Office of Human Rights
Montgomery County Human Relations Commission
Prince George's County Human Relations Commission
Rockville Human Rights Commission

Illegal discrimination: Legislation covers all employers of fifteen or more employees. Discrimination based on the following criteria is against the law: race, color, sex, religion, marital status, age (all ages), national origin, physical or mental disability, pregnancy (treated the same as any other "temporary disability"), and expunged criminal charges. Discrimination claims must be filed within six months of the claimed incident of discrimination.

Blacklisting regulations: None

Plant closing laws: The Maryland state law on plant closings is voluntary and provides recommended guidelines. These suggest ninety days of advance notice for sizable relocations or layoffs unrelated to bankruptcy or labor disputes.

Payment of wages after discharge: Fired employees and employees who quit must be paid by the next regular payday; mine workers must be paid immediately.

Personnel file access: Available for public employees only.

Discharge for wage garnishment: Not allowed for garnishment related to support payments or for any one indebtedness within a calendar year.

Health insurance continuation: Insurance coverage may be continued for six months after termination if the employee was covered for three months prior to termination.

Non-compete agreements: No legislation

Exceptions to at-will employment doctrine: Maryland has been restrictive in recognizing exceptions to the at-will employment doctrine, although it has recognized exceptions in isolated cases. This is one of those states in which the courts seem to dangle the possibility of wrongful discharge suits but rarely side with the fired employee when such a suit arises.

The Maryland courts have said that an *implied contract* can be created by the written language in an employee handbook. However, the language must be explicit in detailing a procedure for termination, and any disclaimer in the handbook will nullify a wrongful discharge suit (that is, it is sufficient for the employer to state in the handbook that all employees are at-will employees or that the handbook cannot be construed to represent an employment contract). As a practical matter, it is thus difficult to use employee handbooks to sue for wrongful discharge.

The state also recognizes *public policy* violations as a basis for litigation, and it is against the law to fire someone in Maryland for making wage or workers' compensation claims, for engaging in legitimate union activity, for filing a safety complaint, or for failing to reveal criminal charges that have been expunged. However, as in the case of the implied contract situation, the courts have interpreted this issue very narrowly and seem to look for very precise violations of public policy. Whistle-blowers who are state employees are theoretically protected, but most of the instances which in other states would have been seen as violations of public policy have in fact been found not to be such by the Maryland courts.

There is no recognition of the *good faith and fair dealing* concept in Maryland.

Massachusetts

EEOC office address:
1 Congress St., 10th Floor
Boston, MA 02114
(617) 565-3200

State enforcement agency:
Massachusetts Commission Against Discrimination
1 Ashburton Place, Ste 601
Boston, MA 02108
(617) 727-3990

Illegal discrimination: Legislation covers all employers of six or more employees. Discrimination based on the following criteria is against the law: race, color, religious creed, national origin, sex, age, ancestry, physical or mental handicap (including AIDS), and sexual orientation. Discrimination claims must be filed within six months of the claimed incident of discrimination.

Blacklisting regulations: None

Plant closing laws: Employers are encouraged in the case of a closing or layoff affecting more than fifty people to give ninety days of advance notice and some continuation of health insurance, but there are no legal requirements. If the company changes hands and more than fifty employees are terminated, and the employee has three or more years of service, and the termination takes place in a time period starting twelve months before the change of control and ending twenty-four months afterward, the new controlling employer must pay severance pay equal to two weeks' pay per year of service, paid in a lump sum.

Payment of wages after discharge: Fired employees must be paid immediately. Employees who quit must be paid by the next regular payday or by the following Saturday.

Personnel file access: Employees have access to their files.

Discharge for wage garnishment: Not allowed for child support garnishment.

Health insurance continuation: Coverage may be continued for up to thirty-nine weeks after termination by the employee paying the appropriate group rate.

Non-compete agreements: No legislation

Exceptions to at-will employment doctrine: As in much other legislation, Massachusetts is one of the most liberal states in recognizing exceptions to the at-will employment doctrine.

The *implied contract* area is one that is somewhat fuzzy. The Massachusetts courts have ruled that an implied contract could be created either by oral statements or by the employee handbook. However, these representations must be specific, and the state courts in a number of cases have refused to treat the employee handbook as a contract. This is quite contrary to the generally employee-oriented nature of Massachusetts courts. If an employee signs an employment agreement specifying that he is an employee at will, oral statements to the contrary will not apply.

The courts also have stated that *public policy* may be a legitimate basis for a wrongful discharge suit. Massachusetts law makes it illegal to fire someone for serving on a jury, for engaging in legitimate union activity, or for filing a wage complaint. As in other states, it must be established that a public policy issue actually is involved in the termination situation. There is no specific whistle-blower protection.

Contrary to the rule in most states, *good faith and fair dealing* cases are quite common in Massachusetts. In a landmark 1977 ruling *(Fortune v. National Cash Register Co.)*, the court stated that an employer did not act in good faith when terminating an employee. This was a case in which a salesman had been fired the day after closing a $5 million order and before his bonus was paid. Although in this extreme case the court found that the employer had not acted in good faith, in other situations in which this concept has been applied the grounds have been quite narrow.

Michigan

EEOC office address:
477 Michigan Ave., Room 1540
Detroit, MI 48226
(313) 226-7636

State enforcement agency:
Michigan Department of Civil Rights
1200 6th Street, 7th Floor
Detroit, MI 48226
(313) 256-2570

Illegal discrimination: Legislation covers all employers of one or more employees. Discrimination based on the following criteria is against the law: race, color, religion, national origin, age (all ages), sex (including pregnancy), height, weight, marital status, and physical or mental handicap (specifically including AIDS). Discrimination claims must be filed within 180 days of the claimed incident of discrimination.

Blacklisting: None

Plant closing laws: There is no required action, but employers are urged to give notification as soon as possible.

Payment of wages after discharge: Fired employees are to be paid immediately. Employees who quit are to be paid as soon as the correct amount can be determined.

Personnel file access: Employees have access to their files but not to reference letters or to medical records.

Discharge for wage garnishment: Discharge based on garnishment alone is forbidden.

Health insurance continuation: No legislation

Non-compete agreements: Allowable if "reasonable"

Exceptions to at-will employment doctrine: Michigan is one of the most liberal states in allowing exceptions to the at-will doctrine, and has been an opinion leader in this regard.

With regard to the *implied contract,* Michigan is the home of *Touissant v. Blue Cross and Blue Shield of Michigan* (1980), the most important employee handbook case in the United States. In this case, the handbook stated that just cause was required for termination and that employees would keep their jobs as long as they performed satisfactorily. Touissant thus was found to have been wrongfully discharged. In this case, the court said that both oral and written statements could in some cases create a contractual relationship between employer and employee. It is clear, however, that statements in the handbook to the effect that all employees are at-will employees will negate the implied contract argument in most cases.

Michigan also recognizes *public policy* violations as criteria for supporting a wrongful discharge claim. The list of circumstances under which firing is not allowed includes: for serving on a jury, for filing a wage or safety complaint, for refusing to take a polygraph test, for legitimate union activity, for whistle-blowing, for filing a workers' compensation claim, and for refusing to falsify a state-required report.

Michigan does not allow for *good faith and fair dealing* as a legal argument; however, because the state has allowed so many other avenues for wrongful discharge cases, this omission is of little consequence.

Minnesota

EEOC office address:
330 2nd Ave. South, Ste 430
Minneapolis, MN 55401
(612) 335-4040

State enforcement agency:
Minnesota Department of Human Rights
500 Bremer Tower
7th Place and Minnesota St.
St. Paul, MN 55101
(612) 296-5663

Illegal discrimination: Legislation covers all employers of one or more employees. Discrimination based on the following criteria is against the law: race, color, creed, religion, national origin, marital status, sex (including pregnancy), participation in public assistance programs, disability (specifically including AIDS), sexual orientation, age (over age 18), nonconviction arrest record, convictions if annulled or expunged, and misdemeanors for which jail time is not permitted. Executives may be forced to retire at age 65 if entitled to a pension of $27,000 per year or more. Discrimination claims must be filed within 300 days of the claimed incident of discrimination.

Blacklisting regulations: Prohibited, and punishable by fines or prison sentences.

Plant closing laws: None. Employers are encouraged on a voluntary basis to give as much advance notification as possible.

Payment of wages after discharge: Fired employees except those named below must be paid immediately, though employees who handle money may have their final pay delayed for as long as ten days. Fired sales workers and migrant workers must be paid within three days. Employees who quit must be paid within five days, though slightly different rules apply to sales and migrant workers and employees who handle money. Strikers must be paid on the next regular payday.

Personnel file access: Employees have access to their files, exclusive of letters of reference.

Discharge for wage garnishment: Prohibited if related to support payments. For other forms of indebtedness, discharge is allowed only if there are three or more garnishments in a ninety-day period representing more than one indebtedness.

Health insurance continuation: Coverage may be continued for a terminated employee for a period up to one year if the employee pays the standard group rate.

Non-compete agreements: No legislation

Exceptions to at-will employment doctrine: Minnesota is in the middle of the pack in terms of allowing exceptions to the at-will employment doctrine.

As in many states, Minnesota supports the *implied contract* concept in cases where quite specific language was used in the employee hand-book or orally, for instance, language stating that specific termination practices would be followed or that termination would be only for just cause. However, general promises of long-term employment are not sufficient.

Minnesota also endorses the *public policy* basis for wrongful dis-charge suits. Employees are protected from discharge for legitimate union activity, for filing a workers compensation claim or safety com-plaint, or for testifying with regard to the enforcement of the mini-mum wage law. Whistle-blowers are protected. However, the courts will look carefully to make certain that public policy truly exists in the subject area and that it has been violated.

Good faith and fair dealing generally is not recognized as the basis for wrongful discharge suits in Minnesota.

Mississippi

EEOC office address:
207 West Amite St.
Jackson, MS 39201
(601) 965-4537

State enforcement agency: None

Illegal discrimination: The state of Mississippi is one of the few states with no antidiscrimination legislation other than a basic law covering state employees only.

Blacklisting regulations: Prohibited for railroad, telephone, and tele-graph employees only and punishable by fines, damages, and prison sentences.

Plant closing laws: None

Payment of wages after discharge: No legislation

Personnel file access: Not guaranteed

Discharge for wage garnishment: Forbidden if the garnishment is child support related.

Health insurance continuation: No legislation

Non-compete agreements: No legislation

Exceptions to at-will employment doctrine: Mississippi arguably is the most backward state in the nation when it comes to employee-friendly legislation and court decisions. If you are a fired Mississippi employee, don't count on the success of a wrongful discharge suit.

In Mississippi, the courts have never upheld an *implied contract* claim; that is, unless there is a specific contract of employment, employers may terminate employees for any reason whatsoever or for no reason at all.

Likewise, the Mississippi courts have recognized no at-will exceptions for violations of *public policy*. Even in the subject area treated most sympathetically in other states, the firing of an employee for filing a workers' compensation claim, Mississippi has refused to accept the concept of wrongful discharge. Whistle-blowers are not protected.

Finally, Mississippi courts do not recognize the concept of *good faith and fair dealing* in employer-employee relationships.

Missouri

EEOC office addresses:
625 North Euclid St.
5th Floor
St. Louis, MO 63108
(314) 425-6585

911 Walnut, 10th Floor
Kansas City, MO 64106
(816) 426-5773

State enforcement agency:
Missouri Commission on Human Rights
3315 Truman Blvd.
Jefferson City, MO 65102
(314) 634-9110

Kansas City Human Relations Commission
St. Louis Civil Rights Enforcement Agency

Illegal discrimination: Legislation covers all employers of six or more employees. Discrimination based on the following criteria is against the law: race, color, religion, ancestry, AIDS, age, sex, physical or mental handicap. It is also illegal to fire someone for refusing to abort a fetus. Discrimination claims must be filed within 180 days of the claimed incident of discrimination.

Blacklisting regulations: Prohibited, and punishable by fines or prison sentences.

Plant closing laws: None

Payment of wages after discharge: Fired employees must be paid immediately.

Personnel file access: No legislation

Discharge for wage garnishment: Prohibited if the garnishment is for support payments or for a single indebtedness of any kind.

Health insurance continuation: No legislation

Non-compete agreements: No legislation

Exceptions to at-will employment doctrine: The Missouri courts have been reluctant to create exceptions to the employment at will doctrine and have done so only in very limited circumstances.

There have as yet been no cases in Missouri in which the courts ruled that an *implied contract* was created between employee and employer, whether owing to employee handbooks or oral statements. Certain rulings have been quite specific in denying the application of this concept.

With regard to the *public policy* exception, the Missouri courts have in isolated cases allowed employees to sue for wrongful discharge, but only if a specific statute was violated. This includes cases in which employees were fired for filing workers' compensation claims and for reporting employer violations of safety laws. Again, however, there are a number of cases in which employees tried to sue for wrongful discharge under a more general concept of public policy violation, even though no specific statute was involved, and the courts have rejected this approach. Whistle-blowers are protected if they work for the state.

Missouri also has rejected the premise that employers must exercise *good faith and fair dealing* in their relationships with employees.

Montana

EEOC office address: None. Discrimination claims covered by federal law should be filed with the EEOC office in Denver (see Colorado).

State enforcement agency:
Montana Human Rights Division
1236 6th Ave., Box 1728
Helena, MT 59624
(406) 444-2884

Illegal discrimination: Legislation covers all employers of one or more employees. Discrimination based on the following criteria is against the law: race, creed, religion, color, national origin, age, marital status, physical or mental handicap, sex, and pregnancy. For government employees and state contractors, discrimination based on political beliefs also is against the law. Discrimination claims must be filed within 180 days of the claimed incident of discrimination.

Blacklisting regulations: Prohibited, and punishable by fines or prison sentences.

Plant closing laws: Legislation covers state government agencies only, and is limited in scope.

Payment of wages after discharge: All terminated employees must be paid within three days, except that employees terminated for cause must be paid immediately. Terminated state employees must be paid on the next regular payday or in fifteen days, whichever comes sooner.

Personnel file access: No legislation

Discharge for wage garnishment: Prohibited

Health insurance continuation: No legislation

Non-compete agreements: Not permitted

Exceptions to at-will employment doctrine: Montana is a totally unique state in that in 1987 it passed the Wrongful Discharge from Employment Act. This law essentially eliminates the concept of at-will employment, and says the following:

- After completing a probationary period, employees may be terminated only for "good cause."
- If the employer has any form of written personnel policies (such as an employee handbook), these policies must be followed when a discharge occurs.
- If an employee wins a wrongful discharge suit, lost wages and benefits of up to four years' duration from the date of the discharge may be collected.
- If there is evidence that the employer engaged in fraud or mal-

ice during a termination, employees may collect punitive damages as well.
- Arbitration is encouraged so as to reduce the cost to both parties and the time burden on the courts.

Prior to the enactment of this statute, Montana had in various cases recognized the existence of the three specific exceptions to employment at will: *implied contracts, public policy* violations, and *good faith and fair dealing*. These precedents may be relevant in some future cases, but in general the 1987 statute will apply.

See Appendix II for the full text of the Montana law.

Nebraska

EEOC office address: None. Discrimination claims based on federal law should be filed with the EEOC office in Denver (see Colorado).

State enforcement agency:
Nebraska Equal Opportunity Commission
State Office Building, 5th Floor
301 Centennial Mall South
Lincoln, NB 68509
(402) 471-2024

Lincoln Commission on Human Rights
Omaha Human Relations Department

Illegal discrimination: Legislation covers all employers of fifteen of more employees. Discrimination based on the following criteria is against the law: race, color, religion, sex (including pregnancy), disability, marital status, national origin, AIDS, age between 40 and 70 (for employers of twenty-five or more employees). Discrimination claims must be filed within 180 days of the claimed incident of discrimination.

Blacklisting regulations: No legislation

Plant closing laws: None

Payment of wages after discharge: Fired employees must be paid on the next regular payday or within two weeks, whichever is sooner.

Personnel file access: No legislation

Discharge for wage garnishment: Not allowed for a single indebtedness.

Health insurance continuation: Involuntarily terminated employees may continue their coverage for six months.

Non-compete agreements: No legislation

Exceptions to at-will employment doctrine: Nebraska is a relatively restrictive state when it comes to allowing exceptions to at-will employment.

Successful lawsuits in the state arguing that a breach of an *implied contract* has taken place have been based both on employee handbooks and on oral statements. Companies also have been told that they must follow established or published termination procedures to avoid violating such an implied contract.

Under the *public policy* concept, it is also illegal in Nebraska to fire someone for serving on a jury or for serving as an election official. In general, whistle-blowers are protected. The courts have accepted the general premise that employees may file for wrongful discharge if public policy has been violated.

The Nebraska courts as yet have not allowed the *good faith and fair dealing* concept in support of a wrongful discharge suit.

Nevada

EEOC office address: None. Discrimination claims under federal law should be filed with the EEOC office in Los Angeles (see California).

State enforcement agency:
Nevada Equal Rights Commission
1515 East Tropicana, Ste 590
Las Vegas, NV 89119
(702) 486-7161

Illegal discrimination: Legislation covers all employers of fifteen or more employees. Discrimination based on the following criteria is against the law: race, color, religion, sex, age, AIDS, physical handicap (including hearing and visual impairment), national origin, and pregnancy. Discrimination claims must be filed with the state within 180 days of the claimed incident of discrimination.

Blacklisting regulations: Prohibited, and punishable by fines and prison sentences.

Plant closing laws: None

Payment of wages after discharge: Fired employees must be paid immediately. Employees who quit must be paid by the next regular payday.

Personnel file access: Available to employees; the law states that access is to records used to confirm qualifications or used as a basis for disciplinary action. Reference letters are not included.

Discharge for wage garnishment: Prohibited when related to child support.

Health insurance continuation: No legislation

Non-compete agreements: No legislation, but these agreements have proved to be virtually unenforceable by employers in the state courts.

Exceptions to at-will employment doctrine: Nevada has been relatively open-minded in allowing exceptions to at-will employment.

The state has allowed wrongful discharge suits under the *implied contract* doctrine on the basis of both employee handbooks and oral statements. It is one of the few states to say that an implied contract may be created even during an employee's initial probationary period (*Stone v. Mission Bay Mortgage Co.*, 1983).

Nevada courts have also recognized that violation of *public policy* can be the basis for a wrongful discharge. Employees may not be fired for filing workers' compensation claims or safety complaints or for refusing to take a polygraph test. An employee also may not be fired on the basis of the report of a "spotter" (someone hired to observe employees at work) without a hearing. There have been very few cases with regard to whistle-blowers, and the state has not yet created this exception to at-will employment.

Good faith and fair dealing has not been established as a requirement in employer-employee relationships.

New Hampshire

EEOC office address: None. Discrimination claims under federal law must be filed with the EEOC office in Boston (see Massachusetts).

State enforcement agency:
New Hampshire Commission for Human Rights
163 Loudon Rd.
Concord, NH 03301
(603) 271-2767

Illegal discrimination: Legislation covers all employers of six or more employees. Discrimination based on the following criteria is against the law: age (all ages), race, sex (including pregnancy), color, marital status, physical or mental disability, religious creed, and national origin. Discrimination claims must be filed within 180 days of the claimed incident of discrimination.

Blacklisting regulations: None

Plant closing laws: None

Payment of wages after discharge: Fired employees must be paid within three days. Employees who quit, are laid off, or go on strike must be paid by the next regular payday.

Personnel file access: Available to all employees.

Discharge for wage garnishment: Prohibited

Health insurance continuation: Employees who have been members of the health insurance plan for at least two months may get continued coverage for thirty-nine weeks by paying the group rate.

Non-compete agreements: No legislation

Exceptions to at-will employment doctrine: New Hampshire has been one of the most forward-looking states in finding exceptions to the at-will doctrine, and has been the source of some landmark law. In the 1974 case *Monge v. Beebe Rubber Co.*, the New Hampshire courts recognized the concept of wrongful discharge in a case where an employee claimed to have been terminated for refusing the sexual advances of her boss. The court held that discharges that can be attributed to bad faith, malice, or retaliation are unlawful, thus creating the *good faith and fair dealing* exception to at-will employment.

The New Hampshire courts have also given very broad interpretation to the concept of *public policy* violation, including a statement that public policy need not be expressed in a specific state law. Virtually every other state insists on the existence of a statute that specifically has been violated by the termination. Here again the state has helped create an underlying principle that has been used elsewhere, starting with *Cloutier v. The Great Atlantic and Pacific Tea Company* (1981). Whistle-blowers too are protected.

The *implied contract* concept has also been established.

New Jersey

EEOC office address:
1 Newark Center, Ste 2132
Newark, NJ 07102
(201) 645-6383

State enforcement agency:
New Jersey Department of Law and Public Safety
Division on Civil Rights
383 West State St.
Trenton, NJ 08625
(609) 984-3100

Illegal discrimination: Legislation covers all employers of one or more employees. Discrimination based on the following criteria is against the law: race, color, creed, national origin, ancestry, age (all ages), sex, affectional or sexual orientation, marital status, nationality, liability for military service, atypical hereditary cellular or blood trait, and physical or mental handicap (specifically including AIDS). Discrimination claims must be filed within 180 days of the claimed incident of discrimination.

Blacklisting regulations: None

Plant closing laws: None

Payment of wages after discharge: All terminated employees must be paid by the next regular payday.

Personnel file access: No legislation, but the New Jersey Supreme Court has upheld the right of employees to see their files in certain circumstances.

Discharge for wage garnishment: Not permitted

Health insurance continuation: No legislation

Non-compete agreements: No legislation

Exceptions to at-will employment doctrine: Although most large urban states tend toward the liberal side in allowing exceptions to the at-will employment doctrine, New Jersey is about in the middle of the pack. The state does, however, have a very long list of illegal discrimination criteria.

The New Jersey courts have allowed employees to sue for wrongful discharge based on the idea that an employee handbook can create an *implied contract*. However, the courts have also made clear that a disclaimer in the handbook to the effect that the handbook creates no such contract is sufficient to protect the employer from wrongful discharge claims under the implied contract principle. With regard to oral contracts, the courts have stated that an oral guarantee of lifetime employment may be enforceable *(Shebar, 544 A.2d 377, N.J. 1988)*.

New Jersey also has a statute that prevents employee discharges in cases where the employee discloses or threatens to disclose practices that violate *public policy*, that is, whistle-blowers are protected. This is unusual in that most states have established this principle via court cases rather than through the legislature. The law also says that it is illegal to retaliate against an employee for testifying before a government entity or for refusing to participate in acts the employee believes to be illegal, fraudulent, or in violation of other public policy. Employees also may not be fired for filing a workers' compensation claim.

The New Jersey courts generally have not accepted the concept of *good faith and fair dealing* in termination situations. However, in *Nolan (579 A.2d 1252, N.J. App. 1990)*, the courts supported this concept with regard to the arbitrary changing of a sales compensation plan, so there may be an opening for broader application of the concept.

New Mexico

EEOC office address:
505 Marquette, N.W., Ste 900
Albuquerque, NM 87102
(505) 766-2061

State enforcement agency:
New Mexico Department of Labor
Human Rights Division
Aspen Plaza, 1596 Pacheco St.
Santa Fe, NM 87502
(505) 827-6838

Illegal discrimination: Legislation covers all employers of four or more employees. Discrimination based on the following criteria is against the law: race, age (all ages, though compulsory retirement at age 65 is allowed), religion, color, national origin, ancestry, sex, physical or mental handicap, medical condition (specifically cancer), and AIDS.

Discrimination claims must be filed within 180 days of the claimed incident of discrimination.

Backlisting regulations: Prohibited, and punishable by fines and prison sentences.

Plant closing laws: None

Payment of wages after discharge: Fired employees must be paid within five days. Employees who quit or go on strike must be paid by the next regular payday.

Personnel file access: No legislation

Discharge for wage garnishment: Not allowed if the garnishment is for child support payments.

Health insurance continuation: Employees may continue coverage for six months at the group rate.

Non-compete agreements: No legislation

Exceptions to at-will employment doctrine: New Mexico has at-will rules similar to those in many states in that its courts have recognized the two most common exceptions. However, the courts have made the requirements for these exceptions more restrictive than average, so New Mexico must be considered a more-difficult-than-average state in which to win a wrongful discharge suit.

The state courts have recognized that an employee handbook can form an *implied contract* between employer and employee. However, the wording in the handbook is of paramount importance in that it must be very specific. For example, wording to the effect that "repeated warnings" were required for a discharge and that a discharge without warning could only be "for cause" was not regarded as having created a contract; this is a quite restrictive interpretation of handbook wording (*Walter Sanchez v. The New Mexican*, 1987).

 Public policy violations have also been accepted as the basis for wrongful discharge suits. As in many other states, employees are theoretically protected from discharge for filing workers' compensation claims and safety complaints. As in the implied contract case, however, the New Mexico courts have required quite specific violations of public policy to enforce wrongful discharge rather than accept the broader interpretation available in some other states. No broad whistle-blower statute exists.

 There has been no enforcement of the requirement that employers practice *good faith and fair dealing* with their employees.

New York

EEOC office addresses:

7 World Trade Center
18th Floor
New York, NY 10048
(212) 748-8500

6 Fountain Plaza, Ste 350
Buffalo, NY 14203
(716) 846-4441

State enforcement agency:
New York Division of Human Rights
55 West 125th St.
New York, NY 10027
(212) 870-8400

Illegal discrimination: Legislation covers all employers of four or more employees. Discrimination based on the following criteria is against the law: age (18 or older), race, creed, color, sex, national origin, physical or mental disability (including AIDS and substance abuse), and marital status. Discrimination claims must be filed within one year of the claimed incident of discrimination.

Blacklisting regulations: Blacklisting is prohibited.

Plant closing laws: New York merely has voluntary guidelines that are not enforced in any way. Employers can join a state cooperative that requires that advance notice be given in the case of plant closings; if they are members and give such notice, the employer is eligible for some types of state economic assistance.

Payment of wages after discharge: Employees who quit or are fired must be paid by the next regular payday.

Personnel file access: No legislation

Discharge for wage garnishment: Prohibited

Health insurance continuation: No legislation

Non-compete agreements: No legislation

Exceptions to at-will employment doctrine: Somewhat surprisingly, New York, unlike most large urban states, has relatively restrictive policies regarding exceptions to employment at will.

The state courts have recognized that written or oral statements may create an *implied contract* between employer and employee. This has been applied to employee handbooks (though reluctantly and not frequently), to application forms, and to statements made by interviewers during the hiring process and by supervisors after hiring has taken place. The courts have proved especially sympathetic in cases where an employee was induced to leave one employer for another with such promises and then was later discharged.

Although New York does have a whistle-blower law, it is a narrow one, requiring that it apply to situations where the illegal activity would pose a "substantial and specific danger to the public health or safety." The state has consistently refused to recognize the broader concept of *public policy* violation as the basis for wrongful discharge suits, and is one of the relatively few states to take this position. New York laws theoretically protect employees from discharge for serving on a jury, for responding to a subpoena, for reporting violations of labor law, for reporting an employer's illegal or dangerous activities, for engaging in legitimate union activity, or for filing a workers' compensation claim, but the courts have not treated these as the basis for wrongful discharge lawsuits.

The New York courts have not required *good faith and fair dealing* in employer-employee relationships.

North Carolina

EEOC office addresses:
5500 Central Ave.
Charlotte, NC 28212
(704) 567-7100

801 Summit Ave.
Greensboro, NC 27405
(919) 333-5174

1309 Annapolis Drive
Raleigh, NC 27608
(919) 856-4064

State enforcement agency:
North Carolina Human Relations Commission
121 West Jones St.
Raleigh, NC 27603
(919) 733-7996

The Raleigh Human Resources Department and the New Hanover Human Relations Commission also will act as 706 agencies in some situations.

Illegal discrimination: North Carolina only very recently passed antidiscrimination laws, applying to all employers of fifteen or more employees. Discrimination based on the following criteria is against the law:

race, color, religion, age, national origin, physical or mental disability, and AIDS.

Blacklisting regulations: Prohibited, and punishable by fines and damages.

Plant closing laws: None

Payment of wages after discharge: All terminated employees must be paid by the next regular payday.

Personnel file access: Employees have limited access for the purpose of examining certain health and safety information, but there is no general access to files.

Discharge for wage garnishment: Not permitted if the garnishment is for child support.

Health insurance continuation: Employees who were members of the health insurance plan for at least three months before termination may continue coverage for three months at the group rate.

Non-compete agreements: No legislation. The North Carolina Supreme Court has allowed non-compete agreements of up to two years' duration.

Exceptions to at-will employment doctrine: In spite of the lack of laws relating to employment discrimination, North Carolina in recent years has moved out of the Dark Ages into recognizing some exceptions to the at-will employment doctrine. However, it must still be considered a poor environment for wrongful discharge suits if you are the discharged employee.

As a result of *Sides v. Duke Hospital* (1985), the North Carolina courts recognized both the *implied contract* concept (in this case based on promises made during the job interview) and the *public policy* exception to at-will employment. The public policy issue in this case involved a nurse who was fired for refusing to testify falsely in a malpractice suit, and the courts in this state have been slow to expand the public policy issue beyond the perjury example. Likewise, with regard to implied contracts, the state courts have thus far not accepted the wording in employee handbooks as grounds for wrongful discharge suits.

North Carolina law protects employees who file workers' compensation claims, who serve on a jury, or who testify before or aid certain government officials in legal proceedings. State employees have whistle-blower protection.

As yet, the North Carolina courts have not allowed the *good faith and fair dealing* concept as a basis for a wrongful discharge suit.

North Dakota

EEOC office address: None. Discrimination claims under federal law should be directed to the EEOC office in Denver (see Colorado).

State enforcement agency:
North Dakota Department of Labor
600 East Blvd.
Bismarck, ND 58505
(701) 224-2660

Illegal discrimination: Legislation covers all employers of ten or more employees. Discrimination based on the following criteria is against the law: race, color, religion, sex, national origin, age, physical or mental handicap (specifically including AIDS), marital status, and public assistance status. Mandatory retirement for high-level executives at age 65 is legal if they are entitled to an annual pension of $44,000 or more.

Blacklisting regulations: Prohibited, and punishable by fines or prison sentences.

Plant closing laws: None

Payment of wages after discharge: Fired employees must be paid within one day. Employees who quit or go on strike must be paid by the next regular payday.

Personnel file access: Available to government employees only.

Discharge for wage garnishment: Prohibited

Health insurance continuation: Terminated employees who have been covered by health insurance at their employer for three months or longer may continue coverage for up to thirty-nine weeks at the group rate.

Non-compete agreements: No legislation, but these agreements have proved to be virtually unenforceable by employers when tested in the courts.

Exceptions to at-will employment doctrine: North Dakota is relatively restrictive when it comes to finding exceptions to the at-will employment doctrine.

The state courts have on occasion recognized that an *implied contract* can be created by an employee handbook. However, a statement in the handbook to the effect that no contract is created by the handbook is sufficient to eliminate this problem for employers and to defuse a wrongful discharge suit.

The courts have not as yet recognized violations of *public policy* as the basis for wrongful discharge suits, although certain statutes make it illegal to discharge or to retaliate against an employee for serving on a jury or filing a wage complaint. Whistle-blowers who are state employees are protected.

Good faith and fair dealing has not been established as the basis for wrongful discharge suits in this state.

Ohio

EEOC office addresses:
1660 West 2nd St., Ste 850
Cleveland, OH 44113
(216) 522-2001

525 Vine St., Ste 810
Cincinnati, OH 45202
(513) 684-2851

State enforcement agency:
Ohio Civil Rights Commission
220 Parsons Ave.
Columbus, OH 43266
(614) 466-2785

The OCRC also has offices in Cleveland, Dayton, Toledo, Akron, and Cincinnati.

Springfield Human Relations Department
Youngstown Human Relations Commission

Illegal discrimination: Legislation covers all employers of four or more employees. Discrimination based on the following criteria is against the law: race, color, religion, sex (including pregnancy), national origin, physical or mental handicap (specifically including AIDS), age, and ancestry. Mandatory retirement at age 65 is acceptable for high-level executives who will receive a pension of at least $44,000 per year. Discrimination claims must be filed with the state within six months of the claimed incident of discrimination.

Blacklisting regulations: None

Plant closing laws: None

Payment of wages after discharge: No legislation

Personnel file access: Available for medical records only.

Discharge for wage garnishment: Not allowed for a single garnishment in a twelve-month period or for garnishment for child support.

Health insurance continuation: Terminated employees who have been covered by health insurance for at least three months prior to termination may continue coverage at the group rate for six months.

Non-compete agreements: No legislation

Exceptions to at-will employment doctrine: The Ohio courts have been somewhat more open than courts in the average state to permitting exceptions to the employment at-will doctrine.

Employee handbook statements have been interpreted as creating an *implied contract* and allowed to be used as the basis for a wrongful discharge suit. In *Stearns v. Ohio Savings Assn.* (1984), the court also said that someone who had been induced away from another job with a promise of an annual salary in effect had received a one-year employment contract. Employers can protect themselves by including a statement in the handbook to the effect that employees are employed at will and that no contractual obligation is created by any wording in the handbook.

Ohio statutes make it illegal to fire someone for serving on a jury, and retaliation is not permitted against employees who file wage complaints or workers' compensation claims. In a more general sense, the courts have accepted the *public policy* violation concept, but will look for a clearly stated statute that has been violated. Whistle-blowers are protected by statute.

The courts as yet have not recognized *good faith and fair dealing* as a basis for wrongful discharge suits.

Oklahoma

EEOC office address:
531 Couch Drive
Oklahoma City, OK 73102
(405) 231-4911

State enforcement agency:
Oklahoma Human Rights Commission
Jim Thorpe Building, Room 480
2101 North Lincoln Blvd.
Oklahoma City, OK 73105
(405) 521-2360

Illegal discrimination: Legislation covers all employers of fifteen or more employees. Discrimination based on the following criteria is against the law: race, color, religion, sex, national origin, age 40 or older, physical or mental handicap. Mandatory retirement of high-level executives at age 65 is legal if they will receive a pension of at least $44,000 per year. Discrimination claims must be filed with the state within 180 days of the claimed incident of discrimination.

Blacklisting regulations: Prohibited, and punishable by fines and damages.

Plant closing laws: None

Payment of wages after discharge: All terminated employees must be paid by the next regular workday.

Personnel file access: Available for medical records only.

Discharge for wage garnishment: Not allowed for child support garnishment or for two or fewer garnishments in a single year.

Health insurance continuation: Terminated employees with at least six months of prior coverage automatically get thirty days of continuation coverage and can get three additional months of basic coverage and six months of major medical coverage by paying the group rate.

Non-compete agreements: Not allowed

Exceptions to at-will employment doctrine: Oklahoma is somewhat more open-minded than the average state in allowing wrongful discharge suits based on exceptions to at-will employment.

The state courts have recognized that an employee handbook can create an *implied contract*. However, the employee must be able to prove that he or she read the handbook prior to termination and was assuming that the provisions in the handbook were in force.

State law makes it illegal to discharge employees for serving on a jury, or to retaliate against an employee for filing a workers' compensation claim. Whistle-blowers have been protected in some instances, but there is no broad statute. In general, the state courts have been quite open to *public policy* violations as constituting a basis for wrong-ful discharge suits.

The courts have been far less willing to consider *good faith and fair dealing* as a requirement for employers. One case in which this concept was upheld involved a salesman who was fired without good cause and lost commissions as a result, but the courts generally have taken the position that public policy must be violated for the concept of bad faith to be introduced.

Oregon

EEOC office address: None. Discrimination claims under federal law must be filed with the EEOC office in Seattle (see Washington).

State enforcement agency:
Bureau of Labor and Industries
Civil Rights Division
800 N.E. Oregon St., Ste 32
Portland, OR 97232
(503) 731-4075

Illegal discrimination: Legislation covers all employers of one or more employees. Discrimination based on the following criteria is against the law: race, religion, color, sex (including pregnancy), national origin, marital status, age (18 or older), expunged juvenile record, and family relationship with another employee of the same company unless one exerts supervisory responsibility or grievance control with regard to the other. For employers with six or more employees, discrimination based on physical or mental handicaps (including AIDS) also is illegal. Discrimination claims must be filed within one year of the claimed incident of discrimination.

Blacklisting regulations: Prohibited

Plant closing laws: None

Payment of wages after discharge: Fired employees must be paid immediately. Employees who quit must be paid within five working days if they give no notice, and immediately if they give two days of notice. Strikers must be paid on the next regular payday or within thirty days, whichever is sooner.

Personnel file access: Available to all employees.

Discharge for garnishment: Prohibited

Health insurance continuation: No legislation

Non-compete agreements: Illegal unless they were negotiated at the time of hiring or at the time of a promotion.

Exceptions to at-will employment doctrine: Oregon has been relatively open-minded about allowing exceptions to employment at will.

The state courts have accepted the premise that an *implied contract* can be created by the wording of an employee handbook. Case law has centered around handbooks which say that termination will be for just cause only, at which point the court may have to determine if just cause existed in the particular case.

The Oregon courts have recognized several situations in which *public policy* issues may come into play. The Oregon legislature has outlawed discharge of an employee for serving on a jury, for legitimate union activity, for filing a wage or safety complaint, for filing a workers' compensation claim, or for being related to another employee of the same employer. Whistle-blowers are protected. The court has been cautious, however, in situations where the employee was protected under federal law, and has deflected wrongful discharge suits that were adequately covered by other kinds of legislation.

Oregon courts have given basic recognition to the concept of *good faith and fair dealing,* but the principle is not well established.

Pennsylvania

EEOC office addresses:

1421 Cherry St., 10th Floor
Philadelphia, PA 19102
(215) 656-7000

1000 Liberty Ave., Room 2038-A
Pittsburgh, PA 15222
(412) 644-3444

State enforcement agency:
Pennsylvania Human Relations Commission
101 South Second St., Ste 300
P.O. Box 3145
Harrisburg, PA 17105
(717) 787-4410

Allentown Human Relations Commission
Philadelphia Commission on Human Relations
Pittsburgh Commission on Human Relations
York Human Relations Commission

Illegal discrimination: Legislation covers all employers of four or more employees. Discrimination based on the following criteria is against the law: race, color, religious creed, ancestry, age, sex, national origin, pregnancy, non–job-related handicap or disability (physical or mental, including AIDS), use of a guide or support animal because of blindness/deafness/physical handicap, marital status (unless applied equally to both sexes), and parenthood (unless applied equally to both sexes). Public employees are also protected from discrimination on the basis of life-style or sexual preference. Discrimination claims must be filed within 180 days of the claimed incident of discrimination.

Blacklisting regulations: None

Plant closing laws: In Philadelphia only, employers of fifty or more employees must give sixty days notice of a plant closing or relocation.

Payment of wages after discharge: Employees who quit or are fired must be paid by the next regularly scheduled payday.

Personnel file access: Available to all employees, but this does not include access to reference letters or medical records.

Discharge for wage garnishment: Prohibited when the garnishment is support-related.

Health insurance continuation: Terminated employees can convert to individual coverage within thirty-one days of the termination of group coverage.

Non-compete agreements: No legislation

Exceptions to at-will employment doctrine: Pennsylvania courts have been relatively liberal in allowing exceptions to the employment at will doctrine, but by and large Pennsylvania has been friendlier to employers than to employees.

It has been relatively difficult for Pennsylvania employees to get the courts to accept employee handbooks as *implied contracts,* although there have been cases in which the courts have recognized the principle without applying it in that particular case. The courts have been a bit more open in allowing oral promises and past employer practices to create such contracts. For example, in 1991 the state courts decided that leaving one high-level job for another, selling a house, and relocating were sufficient indication that a promise of a seven-year contract had been made and taken seriously by the employee in question, and an exception to the at-will doctrine was allowed and the oral contract was enforced *(Cashdollar, 595 A.2d 70, PA App. 1991).* Overall, the Pennsylvania courts have been more open to the philosophical position that an implied contract can be created than they have been to actually recognizing that one exists.

Public policy violations are well recognized as the basis for wrongful discharge cases, and Pennsylvania was one of the earlier states to accept this principle. It is expressly illegal to discharge an employee because of jury duty, for legitimate union activity, for volunteer fire duty, or for whistle-blowing (the latter category applies to public employees and to employees involved in hazardous, nuclear, or other waste management). In *Novosel v. Nationwide Insurance Co.* (1983), an employee who was fired for refusing to lobby on behalf of no-fault reform was supported by the courts in a wrongful discharge suit based on the principle that an employer may not dictate the political activities of an employee. In general, the Pennsylvania courts have been quite open to the public policy exception.

There is no requirement or case law suggesting that an employer in Pennsylvania must engage in *good faith and fair dealing.*

Rhode Island

EEOC office address: None. Discrimination claims under federal law should be directed to the Boston office (see Massachusetts).

State enforcement agency:
Rhode Island Commission on Human Rights
10 Abbott Park Place
Providence, RI 02903
(401) 277-2661

Illegal discrimination: Legislation covers all employers of four or more employees. Discrimination based on the following criteria is against the law: race, color, religion, sex, physical or mental handicap, age, country of ancestral origin, AIDS, and genetic testing. Discrimination claims must be filed within one year of the claimed incident of discrimination.

Blacklisting regulations: None

Plant closing laws: None

Payment of wages after discharge: Employees who quit or are fired must be paid by the next regular payday. If the employer closes or moves out of state, terminated employees must be paid within twenty-four hours. Employers (of fifty or more employees) who are acquired or in some other way undergo a change of control must pay severance to employees who are terminated within two years of this transfer of control. This severance must be equal to twice the employee's weekly wage multiplied by the number of years of service.

Personnel file access: Available to all employees, but not including letters of reference or medical records.

Discharge for wage garnishment: Illegal if the garnishment is for child support.

Health insurance continuation: Benefits may be extended for up to eighteen months in the case of layoff, death, or plant closure.

Non-compete agreements: No legislation

Exceptions to at-will employment doctrine: The Rhode Island courts have been quite restrictive in wrongful discharge cases, and exceptions to at-will employment are few.

With regard to the *implied contract* concept, the courts have consistently held that only in cases where a length of employment was specifically agreed to in advance can the at-will doctrine be breached. Likewise, there would have to be a specific agreement that termination would be only for just cause.

There are some cases in which *public policy* can be used to create an exception to at-will employment. Rhode Island employers cannot fire an employee for engaging in lawful union activity or for filing a wage complaint. Because employers also may not require an employee to take a polygraph test, it can be inferred that employees cannot be discharged for refusing to take one. Whistle-blowers are protected.

The courts have not recognized *good faith and fair dealing* as a requirement in employer-employee relationships.

South Carolina

EEOC office address:
15 South Main St.
Greenville, SC 29601
(803) 241-4400

State enforcement agency:
South Carolina Human Affairs Commission
2611 Forest Drive, Ste 200
P.O. Box 4490
Columbia, SC 29240
(803) 253-6336

Illegal discrimination: Legislation covers all employers of fifteen or more employees. Discrimination based on the following criteria is against the law: race, color, religion, sex (including pregnancy), age, national origin, and handicap (includes physical or mental impairment but not mental illness). Executive-level employees may be subject to compulsory retirement at age 65 if they are entitled to a pension of $27,000 or more per year. Discrimination claims must be filed within 180 days of the claimed incident of discrimination.

Blacklisting regulations: None

Plant closing laws: In cases where the employer requires advance notice from an employee who is quitting, the employer is required to give at least two weeks of notice before a plant closing.

Payment of wages after discharge: Fired employees must be paid within two days or on the next regular payday. Strikers must be paid on the next regular payday.

Personnel file access: Available only to employees of the state government, and with restrictions.

Discharge for wage garnishment: Illegal for garnishments related to support orders or consumer credit transactions.

Health insurance continuation: For terminated employees who have been covered by the group plan for three months or longer, coverage may be continued for the calendar month of termination plus one additional month at the group rate.

Non-compete agreements: No legislation

Exceptions to at-will employment doctrine: Unlike many states in the Deep South, South Carolina has a reasonably enlightened attitude toward at-will employment.

The state courts have accepted the premise that employee handbooks that outline termination procedures can create an *implied contract,* although a disclaimer in the handbook to the effect that all employees are at-will employees will prevent such a contract from being formed.

Public policy violations as a basis for wrongful discharge suits have also been accepted by the courts. State statutes make it illegal to fire an employee for his or her political activities, for serving on a jury, for complying with a subpoena, or for filing a safety complaint. Whistle-blowers are protected if they are state government employees.

The South Carolina courts have not recognized any requirement for *good faith and fair dealing.*

South Dakota

EEOC office address: None. Discrimination claims under federal law must be filed with the EEOC office in Denver (see Colorado).

State enforcement agency:
South Dakota Division of Human Rights
State Capitol Building
Pierre, SD 57501
(605) 773-4493

Sioux Falls Human Relations Commission

Illegal discrimination: Legislation covers all employers of one or more employees. Discrimination based on the following criteria is against the law: race, color, creed, religion, sex (including pregnancy), ancestry, mental or physical disability, and national origin. Discrimination based on age and political affiliation applies to public employees only. Discrimination claims must be filed within 180 days of the claimed incident of discrimination.

Blacklisting regulations: None

Plant closing laws: None

Payment of wages after discharge: Employees who quit must be paid by the next regular payday or when the employer's property has been returned, whichever is later. Employees who are fired must be paid within five days. Strikers must be paid by the next regular payday.

Personnel file access: Available only to public employees, and not including performance evaluations or employment examinations.

Discharge for wage garnishment: Not permitted if the garnishment is for child support.

Health insurance continuation: For employees who previously have been covered by a group plan for six months, coverage may be continued for six months after termination at the group rate.

Non-compete agreements: Must be no more than two years in duration.

Exceptions to at-will employment doctrine: South Dakota has recognized some tightly defined exceptions to the at-will employment doctrine, but overall it is one of the more restrictive states.

The state courts have recognized that an employee handbook can create an *implied contract* with regard to termination procedures.

Although there is no protection per se for whistle-blowers, the courts have voided a discharge in a situation where an employee was fired for refusing to commit an illegal act. The law also prevents discharge for serving on a jury, for legitimate union activity, and for filing a wage complaint.

Good faith and fair dealing is not required in South Dakota.

Tennessee

EEOC office addresses:

1407 Union Ave., Ste 621
Memphis, TN 38104
(901) 722-2617

50 Vantage Way, Ste 202
Nashville, TN 37228
(615) 736-5820

State enforcement agency:
Tennessee Human Rights Commission
Cornerstone Square Building, Ste 400
530 Church St.
Nashville, TN 37243
(615) 741-5825

Illegal discrimination: Legislation covers all employers of eight or more employees. Discrimination based on the following criteria is against the law: race, creed, color, religion, sex, age, national origin, physical or mental disability, visual handicap, or use of a guide dog. Executives may be required to retire at age 65 if entitled to a pension of $44,000 per year or more. Discrimination claims must be filed within 180 days of the claimed incident of discrimination.

Blacklisting regulations: None

Plant closing laws: In cases of a relocation or closing affecting fifty or more employees in a three-month period, employers are required to give some advance notice.

Payment of wages after discharge: No legislation

Personnel file access: Available to public employees only.

Discharge for wage garnishment: Illegal for support-related garnishment.

Health insurance continuation: For employees previously covered for at least three months under the group plan, coverage may be continued for three months plus the balance of the termination month at the group rate.

Non-compete agreements: No legislation

Exceptions to at-will employment doctrine: Tennessee is one of the most conservative states with regard to allowing exceptions to at-will employment.

The *implied contract* exception to at-will employment has been allowed only in cases of a written employment contract specifying a term of employment; the phrase *lifetime employment* is considered meaningless because "lifetime" is not a specific term of employment, and such employees are employees at will. Oral promises of any term of employment will not stand up in court.

   Whistle-blowers are protected, and employees may not be discharged for filing a workers' compensation claim. In general, however, the Tennessee courts have been unsympathetic to *public policy* violations being used as the basis for exceptions to employment at will. Tennessee is one of the most restrictive states in this area.

   Good faith and fair dealing has no standing as a concept in the state of Tennessee.

Texas

EEOC office addresses:

207 South Houston St.
3rd Floor
Dallas, TX 74202
(214) 655-3355

The Commons, Building C
Ste 100
4171 North Mesa St.
El Paso, TX 79902
(915) 534-6550

1919 Smith St.
7th Floor
Houston, TX 77002
(713) 653-3377

5410 Fredericksburg Rd.
Ste 200
San Antonio, TX 78229
(210) 229-4810

State enforcement agency:
Texas Commission on Human Rights
8100 Cameron Rd., Ste 525
Austin, TX 78754
(512) 837-8534

Austin Human Relations Commission
Corpus Christi Human Relations Commission
Fort Worth Human Relations Commission

Illegal discrimination: Legislation covers all employers of fifteen or more employees. Discrimination based on the following criteria is against the law: race, color, physical or mental disability (not including AIDS), religion, sex (including pregnancy), national origin, and age (40 or older). Mandatory retirement of executives at age 65 is legal if they are entitled to a pension of $27,000 per year or more. Discrimination claims must be filed within 180 days of the claimed incident of discrimination.

Blacklisting regulations: Prohibited, and punishable by fines or prison sentences.

Plant closing laws: None

Payment of wages after discharge: Fired employees must be paid within six days. Employees who quit must be paid by the next regular payday.

Personnel file access: Available to public employees only.

Discharge for wage garnishment: Prohibited when related to child support.

Health insurance continuation: For terminated employees who were covered by group insurance for three months prior to termination, coverage may be converted to individual coverage for thirty-one days after termination. Employees terminated for cause are not covered by this provision.

Non-compete agreements: The Texas courts have in some cases refused to enforce non-compete agreements, such as by declaring that customer lists are not trade secrets. In general, however, non-compete agreements have been allowed and enforced if they contain reasonable limitations as to time, geography, and the nature of the activity.

Exceptions to at-will employment doctrine: Texas courts have been relatively restrictive in finding exceptions to the at-will employment rule, although there have been exceptions to at-will employment in all three broad categories.

With one exception, employee handbooks and oral promises have not been allowed to create an *implied contract* in Texas. The exception is that if an employee handbook spells out a very specific procedure for termination and states that termination will be only for just cause, the courts will allow wrongful discharge suits if these procedures have not been followed.

Texas law makes it illegal to fire an employee for serving on a jury or for filing a workers' compensation claim. There is no specific whistle-blower protection other than for public employees, but the courts have ruled that employees may not be fired for refusing to perform an illegal act, and have stated that whistle-blowers may be protected in some cases.

Although the Texas courts have not addressed the subject of *good faith and fair dealing* per se, they have supported the idea that an employee who is fired for the purpose of depriving him of a bonus payment may have a basis for a wrongful discharge suit.

Utah

EEOC office address: None. Discrimination claims under federal law must be filed at the EEOC office in Phoenix (see Arizona).

State enforcement agency:
Utah Industrial Commission
Anti-Discrimination Division
160 East 3rd South
P.O. Box 146640
Salt Lake City, UT 84114
(801) 530-6801

Illegal discrimination: Legislation covers all employers of fifteen or more employees. Discrimination based on the following criteria is against the law: race, color, sex, age, pregnancy, childbirth, religion, national origin, physical or mental handicap. Mandatory retirement for executives at age 65 is legal if the individual is entitled to a pension of at least $44,000 per year. Discrimination claims must be filed within 180 days of the claimed incident of discrimination.

Blacklisting regulations: Prohibited, and punishable by fines or prison sentences.

Plant closing laws: None

Payment of wages after discharge: Fired employees must be paid within one day. Employees who quit must be paid within three days, or immediately if they gave seventy-two hours' notice. Strikers must be paid by the next regular payday.

Personnel file access: Available to public employees only.

Discharge for wage garnishment: Illegal if garnishment is based on a single indebtedness or on child support payments.

Health insurance continuation: No legislation

Non-compete agreements: No legislation

Exceptions to at-will employment doctrine: Utah has been moderately progressive in recognizing exceptions to at-will employment.

The Utah Supreme Court has accepted the premise that an employee handbook which spelled out a procedure for dismissals has created an *implied contract,* and that an employee could sue for wrongful discharge when this procedure was not followed. In general, employee handbooks have been accepted as creating implied contracts.

Utah also protects whistle-blowers if they are public employees, and recognizes a variety of *public policy* violations as exceptions to the at-will employment doctrine. Employees may not be terminated for refusing to take a polygraph test, for engaging in legitimate union activity, or for filing a safety complaint.

The Utah courts have not expressly addressed the concept of *good faith and fair dealing* in employer-employee relationships.

Vermont

EEOC office address: None. Discrimination claims under federal law must be filed with the EEOC office in Boston (see Massachusetts).

State enforcement agency:
Vermont Attorney General's Office (for employees of private employers)
Civil Rights Division
109 State St.
Montpelier, VT 05609
(802) 828-3171

Vermont Human Rights Commission (for state employees)
133 State St.
Montpelier, VT 05633
(802) 828-2480

Illegal discrimination: Legislation covers all employers of one or more employees. Discrimination based on the following criteria is against the law: race, color, religion, ancestry, national origin, sex, sexual orientation, place of birth, age (18 or older), handicap, and AIDS.

Blacklisting regulations: None

Plant closing laws: None

Payment of wages after discharge: Fired employees must be paid within three days. Employees who quit must be paid by the next regular payday.

Personnel file access: Available to public employees only.

Discharge for wage garnishment: Prohibited

Health insurance continuation: Terminated employees who have been covered for the previous three months by the group insurance plan may continue coverage at the group rate for up to six months.

Non-compete agreements: No legislation

Exceptions to at-will employment doctrine: Vermont has taken relatively restrictive positions with regard to the employment at-will doctrine. This is somewhat unexpected in that Vermont is one of the more liberal states with regard to antidiscrimination legislation.

The *implied contract* exception has been allowed only if the employer and employee have negotiated a specific exception to the at-will doctrine, for example, an employment contract specifying the length of employment. The general terms of an employee handbook are not considered as creating such an exception, although fired employees have won a few lawsuits based on handbook promises.

Public employee whistle-blowers are protected via their union contract, but the courts have been reluctant to create the *public policy* exception to at-will employment. The legislature has created some such exceptions, making it illegal to fire an employee for legitimate union activity or for filing a wage or safety complaint.

The Vermont courts do not recognize *good faith and fair dealing* as the basis for wrongful discharge suits.

Virginia

EEOC office addresses:
3600 West Broad St.
Room 229
Richmond, VA 23230
(804) 771-2692

252 Monticello Ave.
1st Floor
Norfolk, VA 23510
(804) 441-3470

State enforcement agency:
Virginia Council on Human Rights
P.O. Box 717
Richmond, VA 23206
(804) 225-2292

Alexandria Human Rights Office
Fairfax County Human Rights Commission
Arlington County Human Rights Commission
Prince William County Human Rights Commission

Illegal discrimination: Legislation covers all employers. Discrimination based on the following criteria is against the law: race, color, religion, national origin, sex, age, marital status, physical or mental disability. Discrimination claims must be filed within 180 days of the claimed incident of discrimination.

Blacklisting regulations: Prohibited, and punishable by fines.

Plant closing laws: None

Payment of wages after discharge: Fired employees and employees who quit must be paid by the next regular payday.

Personnel file access: None

Discharge for wage garnishment: Illegal if based on garnishment for a single indebtedness or for delinquent child support.

Health insurance continuation: No legislation

Non-compete agreements: No legislation. The Virginia Supreme Court has approved some such agreements when they have not exceeded two years' duration.

Exceptions to at-will employment doctrine: Virginia has been willing to recognize certain exceptions to at-will employment, and in general is about average when compared with other states in this regard.

The courts have found that statements in employee handbooks and oral statements from employer representatives could in theory create an *implied contract,* and have allowed wrongful discharge suits based on these grounds.

The Virginia courts have not recognized *public policy* violations per se as a basis for exceptions to the at-will doctrine. However, there are court cases protecting some whistle-blowers in the state, and it is illegal to discharge an employee for serving on a jury or for filing a safety complaint or workers' compensation claim.

There has been no acknowledgement of *good faith and fair dealing* as a basis for wrongful discharge suits.

Washington

EEOC office address:
909 1st Ave., Ste 400
Seattle, WA 98104
(206) 220-6883

State enforcement agency:
Washington State Human Rights Commission
Evergreen Plaza Building
711 South Capitol Way, Ste 402
P.O. Box 42490
Olympia, WA 98504
(206) 753-6771

Seattle Human Rights Commission
Tacoma Human Rights Commission

Illegal discrimination: Legislation covers all employers of eight or more employees. Discrimination based on the following criteria is against the law: age, sex, marital status, race, creed, color, national origin, handicap (sensory, mental, or physical, including AIDS), and usually criminal conviction history. Discrimination claims must be filed within six months of the claimed incident of discrimination.

Blacklisting regulations: Prohibited

Plant closing laws: None

Payment of wages after discharge: Fired employees and employees who quit must be paid by the next regular payday.

Personnel file access: Available to all employees.

Discharge for wage garnishment: Prohibited if the garnishment is for child support. Discharge also is prohibited unless there are three or more garnishments within a twelve-month period.

Health insurance continuation: No legislation

Non-compete agreements: No legislation

Exceptions to at-will employment doctrine: Washington has been moderately liberal in allowing exceptions to the at-will employment doctrine.

In a 1984 case *(Thompson v. St. Regis Paper)*, the state courts expressly prohibited the concept of *good faith and fair dealing* in employer-employee relationships. At the same time, they recognized the concept of an *implied contract* having been created by statements in an employee handbook. In a later case, the courts even declared that an employee handbook which explicitly states that employees are at-will employees can be overridden by oral statements by company personnel.

The state also accepts that wrongful discharge may have taken place in the case of a *public policy* violation. Although the state whistle-blower law applies only to government employees, the legislature has said that employees who file safety complaints or wage complaints are protected. The courts have also protected an individual who was fired for following the mandates of a federal law.

West Virginia

EEOC office address: None. Discrimination claims under federal law should be addressed to the EEOC office in Philadelphia (see Pennsylvania).

State Enforcement Agency:
West Virginia Human Rights Commission
1321 Plaza East
Charleston, WV 25301
(304) 558-2616

Charleston Human Rights Commission
Wheeling Human Rights Commission

Illegal discrimination: Legislation covers all employers of twelve or more employees. Discrimination based on the following criteria is against the law: race, religion, color, national origin, ancestry, sex, pregnancy, age, blindness, physical or mental disability. Discrimination claims must be filed within 180 days of the claimed incident of discrimination.

Blacklisting regulations: None

Plant closing laws: None

Payment of wages after discharge: Fired employees must be paid within three days. Employees who quit must be paid by the next regular payday unless the employee gives notice of a full pay period or longer, in which case the employee must be paid immediately upon departure. Employees laid off must be paid by the next regular payday.

Personnel file access: No legislation

Discharge for wage garnishment: Not permitted

Health insurance continuation: Employees who were covered for at least three months before termination may continue coverage for eighteen months at the group rate.

Non-compete agreements: No legislation

Exceptions to at-will employment doctrine: West Virginia is quite restrictive in allowing exceptions to the at-will employment doctrine.

The state courts thus far have generally refused to accept statements in employee handbooks as creating an *implied contract.* Although there is some indication that the courts accept the premise of implied contracts, there have been only one or two specific situations in which such a contract has been upheld.

The courts have accepted that certain types of *public policy* violations can form the basis for a wrongful discharge suit. Whistle-blowers are protected if they are state employees, as are employees engaging in legitimate union activities and employees who file wage complaints, employees who refuse to take lie detector tests, and employees who file workers' compensation claims.

Employees are not protected by any requirement that employers use *good faith and fair dealing* in their relationships.

Wisconsin

EEOC office address:
310 West Wisconsin Ave., Ste 800
Milwaukee, WI 53203
(414) 297-1111

State enforcement agency:
Wisconsin Department of Industry, Labor and Human Relations
Equal Rights Division
201 East Washington Ave., Room 407
Madison, WI 53702
(or P.O. Box 8928, Madison, WI 53708)

Madison Equal Opportunity Commission
Wisconsin State Personnel Commission (for state employees)

Illegal discrimination: Legislation covers all employers of one or more employees. Discrimination based on the following criteria is against the law: age, race, creed, color, physical or mental handicap (including AIDS), marital status, sex, national origin, ancestry, pregnancy, sexual orientation, arrest or conviction record (unless based on the breaking of a law directly related to the type of employment, or if a bond is required), and membership in the armed forces. Discrimination claims must be filed within 300 days of the claimed incident of discrimination.

Blacklisting regulations: Prohibited, and punishable by fines.

Plant closing laws: Employers of fifty or more employees who close a facility where more than twenty-five employees are affected, or in cases of layoffs where twenty-five or more people (or twenty-five percent of the work force, whichever is greater) are affected, must give sixty days' notice to their employees. This law does not apply to strike or lockout situations.

Payment of wages after discharge: Fired employees must be paid within three days. Employees who quit must be paid within fifteen days. In case of a plant relocation, merger, or closure, employees must be paid within twenty-four hours.

Personnel file access: Available to all employees, but not including letters of reference or records relating to a criminal investigation.

Discharge for wage garnishment: Prohibited for a single indebtedness.

Health insurance continuation: Terminated employees who have been covered by insurance for three months or longer may continue coverage at the group rate for up to eighteen months.

Non-compete agreements: Allowable if reasonable.

Exceptions to at-will employment doctrine: In keeping with the state's generally liberal political climate and with its broad antidiscrimination legislation, Wisconsin has been reasonably liberal in allowing exceptions to at-will employment.

An employee handbook can create an *implied contract* and thus form the basis for a wrongful discharge suit. Interestingly enough, this position was established in a situation where the employer had in fact followed the handbook guidelines and thus the employee's wrongful discharge suit was dismissed, but the courts established the implied contract principle in the process.

Although there is no whistle-blower legislation per se other than for public employees and for employees of solid waste disposal and hazardous waste disposal facilities, there are a number of protections from discharge with regard to *public policy* violations. Employees may not be fired for serving on a jury, for engaging in legitimate union activity, for filing a workers' compensation claim, or for testifying in wage proceedings. Also, the Wisconsin policy is different from that in other states in that wrongful discharge for public policy reasons is considered a breach of contract, so the employee may sue for actual damages (not punitive damages) in addition to lost wages and job reinstatement.

The Wisconsin courts do not recognize the principle of *good faith and fair dealing*.

Wyoming

EEOC office address: None. Discrimination claims under federal law should be directed to the EEOC office in Denver (see Colorado).

State enforcement agency:
Wyoming Fair Employment Commission
U.S. West Building
6101 North Yellowstone
Cheyenne, WY 82002
(307) 777-7262

Illegal discrimination: Legislation covers all employers of two or more employees. Discrimination based on the following criteria is against the law: physical or mental handicap, age, sex, race, creed, color, national origin, and ancestry. Discrimination claims must be filed within ninety days of the claimed incident of discrimination.

Blacklisting regulations: None

Plant closing laws: None

Payment of wages after discharge: Fired employees and employees who quit must be paid within five days. Strikers and laid-off employees must be paid by the next regular payday.

Personnel file access: No legislation

Discharge for wage garnishment: Prohibited if the garnishment is for support payments or for consumer credit transactions.

Health insurance continuation: No legislation

Non-compete agreements: No legislation

Exceptions to at-will employment doctrine: Wyoming has been willing to recognize several exceptions to the at-will employment doctrine, and in general is a bit more liberal than the average state.

Employee handbooks have been accepted as the basis for an *implied contract* when the handbook lays out a termination procedure that has not been followed by the employer. Employers who recognize a transition from "probationary" to "permanent" employee status may have amended the at-will understanding and may have to take special steps to justify a termination.

Wyoming also recognizes the *public policy* exceptions to the at-will doctrine. Whistle-blowers generally are not protected, but it is illegal to discharge an employee for serving on a jury or for filing a safety or wage complaint.

The state courts as yet have not recognized that *good faith and fair dealing* is required in employer-employee relationships.

The Montana Wrongful Discharge Act

Only one state in the nation has formulated a law specifically to deal with wrongful discharges: Montana. Although there have been several efforts to draft a model national law for adoption by the states, this effort has failed thus far. The U.S. Congress also shows no indication of formulating such a law. As a result, the Montana Act is most likely to serve as a model should other states choose to enact similar legislation. For this reason, the act is duplicated here in its entirety.

Note that the law cuts both ways: On the one hand, it provides reasonably severe penalties against employers who violate it; on the other, the violations are quite specific and the awards available are limited so that multimillion-dollar judgments are virtually impossible to obtain except in clear cases of fraud or malice by the employer.

Wrongful Discharge From Employment

39-2-901. Short title.   This part may be cited as the "Wrongful Discharge From Employment Act."

39-2-902. Purpose.   This part sets forth certain rights and remedies with respect to wrongful discharge. Except as limited in this part, employment having no specified term may be terminated at the will of either the employer or the employee on notice to the other for any reason considered sufficient by the terminating party. Except as provided in 39-2-912, this part provides the exclusive remedy for a wrongful discharge from employment.

39-2-903. Definitions.   In this part, the following definitions apply:
    (1) "Constructive discharge" means the voluntary termination of employment by an employee because of a situation created by an act

or omission of the employer which an objective, reasonable person would find so intolerable that voluntary termination is the only reasonable alternative. Constructive discharge does not mean voluntary termination because of an employer's refusal to promote the employee or improve wages, responsibilities, or other terms and conditions of employment.

(2) "Discharge" includes a constructive discharge as defined in subsection (1) and any other termination of employment, including resignation, elimination of the job, layoff for lack of work, failure to recall or rehire, and any other cutback in the number of employees for a legitimate business reason.

(3) "Employee" means a person who works for another for hire. The term does not include a person who is an independent contractor.

(4) "Fringe benefits" means the value of any employer-paid vacation leave, sick leave, medical insurance plan, disability insurance plan, life insurance plan, and pension benefit plan in force on the date of the termination.

(5) "Good cause" means reasonable job-related grounds for dismissal based on a failure to satisfactorily perform job duties, disruption of the employer's operation, or other legitimate business reason.

(6) "Lost wages" means the gross amount of wages that would have been reported to the Internal Revenue Service as gross income on Form W-2 and includes additional compensation deferred at the option of the employee.

(7) "Public policy" means a policy in effect at the time of the discharge concerning the public health, safety, or welfare established by constitutional provision, statute, or administrative rule.

39-2-904. Elements of wrongful discharge. A discharge is wrongful only if:

(1) it was in retaliation for the employee's refusal to violate public policy or for reporting a violation of public policy;

(2) the discharge was not for good cause and the employee had completed the employer's probationary period of employment; or

(3) the employer violated the express provisions of its own written personnel policy.

39-2-905. Remedies.

(1) If an employer has committed a wrongful discharge, the employee may be awarded lost wages and fringe benefits for a period not to exceed 4 years from the date of the discharge, together with interest thereon. Interim earnings, including amounts the employee could

have earned with reasonable diligence, must be deducted from the amount awarded for lost wages.

(2) The employee may recover punitive damages otherwise allowed by law if it is established by clear and convincing evidence that the employer engaged in actual fraud or actual malice in the discharge of the employee in violation of 39-2-904(1).

(3) There is no right under any legal theory to damages for wrongful discharge under this part for pain and suffering, emotional distress, compensatory damages, punitive damages, or any other form of damages, except as provided for in subsections (1) and (2).

39-2-906 through 39-2-910 reserved.

39-2-911. Limitation of actions.

(1) An action under this part must be filed within 1 year after the date of discharge.

(2) If an employer maintains written internal procedures, other than those specified in 39-2-912, under which an employee may appeal a discharge within the organizational structure of the employer, the employee shall first exhaust those procedures prior to filing an action under this part. The employee's failure to initiate or exhaust available internal procedures is a defense to an action brought under this part. If the employer's internal procedures are not completed within 90 days from the date the employee initiates the internal procedures, the employee may file an action under this part and for purposes of this subsection the employer's internal procedures are considered exhausted. The limitation period in subsection (1) is tolled until the procedures are exhausted. In no case may the provisions of the employer's internal procedures extend the limitation period in subsection (1) more than 120 days.

(3) If the employer maintains written internal procedures under which an employee may appeal a discharge within the organizational structure of the employer, the employer shall within 7 days of the date of the discharge notify the discharged employee of the existence of such procedures and shall supply the discharged employee with a copy of them. If the employer fails to comply with this subsection, the discharged employee need not comply with subsection (2).

39-2-912. Exemptions.   This part does not apply to a discharge:

(1) that is subject to any other state or federal statute that provides a procedure or remedy for contesting the dispute. Such statutes include those that prohibit discharge for filing complaints, charges, or claims with administrative bodies or that prohibit unlawful dis-

crimination based on race, national origin, sex, age, handicap, creed, religion, political belief, color, marital status, and other similar grounds.

(2) of an employee covered by a written collective bargaining agreement or a written contract of employment for a specific term.

39-2-913. Preemption of common-law remedies. Except as provided in this part, no claim for discharge may arise from tort or express or implied contract.

39-2-914. Arbitration.

(1) Under a written agreement of the parties, a dispute that otherwise could be adjudicated under this part may be resolved by final and binding arbitration as provided in this section.

(2) An offer to arbitrate must be in writing and contain the following provisions:

(a) A neutral arbitrator must be selected by mutual agreement or, in the absence of agreement, as provided in 27-5-211.

(b) The arbitration must be governed by the Uniform Arbitration Act, Title 27, Chapter 5. If there is a conflict between the Uniform Arbitration Act and this part, this part applies.

(c) The arbitrator is bound by this part.

(3) If a complaint is filed under this part, the offer to arbitrate must be made within 60 days after service of the complaint and must be accepted in writing within 30 days after the date the offer is made.

(4) A party who makes a valid offer to arbitrate that is not accepted by the other party and who prevails in an action under this part is entitled as an element of costs to reasonable attorney fees incurred subsequent to the date of the offer.

(5) A discharged employee who makes a valid offer to arbitrate that is accepted by the employer and who prevails in such arbitration is entitled to have the arbitrator's fee and all costs of arbitration paid by the employer.

(6) If a valid offer to arbitrate is made and accepted, arbitration is the exclusive remedy for the wrongful discharge dispute and there is no right to bring or continue a lawsuit under this part. The arbitrator's award is final and binding, subject to review of the arbitrator's decision under the provisions of the Uniform Arbitration Act.

Index